fP

ALSO BY BRENDON BURCHARD

The Millionaire Messenger

Life's Golden Ticket

The Student Leadership Guide

SEMINARS BY BRENDON BURCHARD

High Performance Academy

Experts Academy

World's Greatest Speaker Training

10X Wealth & Business

Meet Brendon online and receive free training at

www.BrendonBurchard.com

THE
CHARGE

ACTIVATING THE 10 HUMAN DRIVES THAT MAKE YOU FEEL ALIVE

BRENDON BURCHARD

FREE PRESS

NEW YORK   LONDON   TORONTO   SYDNEY   NEW DELHI

Free Press
A Division of Simon & Schuster, Inc.
1230 Avenue of the Americas
New York, NY 10020

First Free Press hardcover edition May 2012

FREE PRESS and colophon are trademarks of Simon & Schuster, Inc.

For information about special discounts for bulk purchases,
please contact Simon & Schuster Special Sales at 1-866-506-1949
or business@simonandschuster.com.

The Simon & Schuster Speakers Bureau can bring authors
to your live event. For more information or to book an event
contact the Simon & Schuster Speakers Bureau at 1-866-248-3049
or visit our website at www.simonspeakers.com.

Designed by Julie Schroeder

Manufactured in the United States of America

1   3   5   7   9   10   8   6   4   2

Library of Congress Cataloging-in-Publication Data

Burchard, Brendon.
The charge : activating the 10 human drives that make you feel alive /
Brendon Burchard.
p. cm.
1. Motivation (Psychology) I. Title.
BF503.B87 2012
153.8—dc23   2012004804

ISBN: 978-1-4516-6753-0
ISBN: 978-1-4516-6773-8 (ebook)

Dedicated to my amazing, loving family,
who always allowed me to chase and live the Charged Life:
Mom, Helen, Bryan, David, and my wonderfully present,
kind, energized, beautiful wife, Denise.
And to Dad—we lost you too soon, Pops,
but we carry your charge forever.

A Note to You, the Reader

As a high-performance coach, speaker, and trainer, I have been blessed to work with truly remarkable people (and I include my audiences) from around the globe. Many of the stories in my book are snapshots or syntheses of my experiences and interactions with clients, audiences, and sometimes friends or family members. Some details are left out or changed because they're not relevant to my desired teaching point. And, in full disclosure, some of the stories have been dramatized. In all cases, I've done my best to convey the essential elements of my friends' and clients' stories and to share examples that will enable you to have your own transformations. I hope you enjoy them.

Also, please know that I am not a medical doctor, licensed psychologist, psychotherapist, psychiatrist, neuroscientist, financial or legal strategist, or anything else that ends with "ist." If anything, I am a student and a servant, and while I happily share what I've learned from these fields, none of the information I share with you is intended, nor should it be construed, to be professional medical, psychological, financial, or legal advice. If you need help in those areas, consult area-specific certified professionals. Neither I nor my publisher—especially, please, not my publisher—is responsible for anything that happens in your life, including anything bad or good that happens as a result of your doing what I advise in this book. Indeed, the whole premise of this book is that your life is what YOU make of it.

In writing this page, I share the first lesson of a Charged Life: we can have fun and engagement in anything we do—even dealing with lawyers.

Godspeed,
Brendon

Contents

We are always getting ready to live,
but never living.

—Ralph Waldo Emerson

Out There

The Charged Life, the truly *lived* life, is not a routine existence in some quaint, picturesque village of safety and certainty. No, the life worth living is *out there,* in the wooded wilds of the unknown, on the craggy battlefields that test our wits and wills in the daily fights with our own demons. It is found during the long onward slog through the storms and strife, when we hear only the whispers and taunts of foes and opponents stronger than we, on the ground where we are knocked sprawling and forced to face our own weaknesses, and on the mountaintops that we reach only because we pitted our every ounce of virtue, strength, character, and courage to keep climbing no matter the slings and arrows flung at our backs or the barriers thrown up before us. It is out there that we come face-to-face with the best in ourselves and with our destiny. It is out there, in a new world of uncertainty and adventure, that we push ourselves, better ourselves, realize ourselves. It is only in the herculean quest for something more that life fills us with wisdom and meaning, but only after we have paid with our sweat and, at times, our tears. It is in the marching on when we are tired and weak and fearful, and in the camaraderie of those fellow warriors we have striven with—our brothers and sisters and family and friends who cheered us on and toiled with us despite the messiness and apparent madness of it all. It is out there on the path less traveled, an uncharted path chosen by each of us alone, an often meandering, overgrown path that leads only to another unpaved road or open field of opportunity, where we must strike out once more with the same hope for victory and transcendence. It is out there when we have the guts to stand naked before the world as who we truly are, when we peer into the souls of those around us and finally see in them the image of the divine, that we plunge ourselves bravely and unconditionally into love that has no bottom or boundary. It is out there, outside the confines of our comforts and the pleasures of our accumulations, beyond our architecture of the routine, that we slip the bonds of our limiting beliefs, soar magnificently above our own shortcomings, and express our highest selves. It is out there, in a world rich with choice and challenge and fear and freedom, that your greatest gifts and adventures await you. Listen. It is out there that destiny calls. Be bold and ready yourself. It is time to charge once again.

—*Brendon Burchard*

Introduction

This book is an unapologetic assault on boredom, distraction, mediocrity, withdrawal, and living a "normal" life. It will directly call into question why you are allowing yourself to live at the energetic level where you currently reside, and it will aggressively challenge you to live a more vibrant, strategic, and engaged life.

In the pages ahead you will find a pragmatic, often counterintuitive guide that cuts through the clutter of bad advice, lays waste to nearly half a century of psychological misunderstanding, and paves a shimmering golden path to one, and only one, destination: a new life that makes you feel truly, fully, magnificently *alive*.

Face it: the emotional energy of the world has flatlined. Over the past forty years, across almost every developed country in the world, the diagnosis of clinical depression has grown nearly tenfold. This, despite the fact that almost every factor we associate with well-being—plentiful food, money, education, safety, access to the arts and health care—is abundant in these societies. Increasingly, people are reporting feelings of restlessness, fatigue, stress, and a sort of unnamable malaise that leaves them too often feeling bored, unsure, or frustrated.

My guess is, you can relate. Like everyone else, you have everything they say you "need"—safety, shelter, sustenance—and yet there are too many days that you don't feel as excited, productive, or fulfilled as you thought you would. At some level, you may sense that you are not fulfilling the promises you've made to yourself or expressing the potential that lives within you. You start each year fired up for the big race, only to finish at a slow trot. Your week is scheduled to the hilt, but deep down you can tell that the work keeping you busy isn't your life's work. You've got the smarts and the soul and the hunger and the will, but all too often you find yourself spinning on a less-than-merry-go-round of doubt and delay. You're connected to everyone and everything online, but you don't feel nearly as connected to the world or to others as you would like. You're waiting for some kind of permission or right timing to live full out every single day. You feel a restless desire for something more.

Well, I'm here to tell you that you *deserve* something more. But there's a catch: to get it, you're going to have to demand more of yourself. Those words might discourage you or even stop you dead from reading on, I know. You're already fighting hard to stay afloat and awake, hammered by a tough economy, unreasonable demands from every quarter, and not enough sleep. Probably the last thing you want to hear is that you've got to try harder, work smarter, or give more in life.

The problem is, you do. And whether it makes me popular or not, I'm going to challenge you in these pages—and I hope you let me and then rise to the challenge, because I think you know there actually *is* more for you out there. I think you've tasted plenty of magically happy, engaged, and satisfying moments in your life and are willing to do what it takes to enjoy more of them. You can remember times when you had more fun, when you were wild and carefree and felt more excited and hopeful than you ever imagined possible. In short, you've already had a glimpse, a taste, of the Charged Life—a heightened existence that makes you feel energized, engaged, and enthusiastic about living.

If that's true, then let me show you my cards: I don't think the restlessness, boredom, anxiety, fear, or any other enduring negative emotion you may feel about yourself, others, or life in general has anything to do with the economy, the evermore chaotic world we live in, your childhood, bad luck, or any other easy excuse that the propagators of victimhood are handing out these days. No, any lack of charge in your life is only the result of a colossal failure in *strategy*. Only the failure to strategically control the contents of your consciousness keeps you from feeling the consistent internal charge of being fully alive, engaged, connected, and fulfilled. The good news is, you now hold in your hands a very strategic book.

I'm convinced that you've felt a spark in life before, one that lit you up for days. But I don't want just to give you back an emotional charge you may have sensed once or twice before—that would be the sort of cheap trick you could expect from a carnival hypnotist. I want to show you an entirely new plane of possibility and emotional vibrancy that you never knew existed. A more vital, more colorful, more exciting, sexier reality can be yours.

To help people reach that kind of existence, I've spent fifteen years intricately studying everything I could get my hands on in the fields of psychology, neuroscience, human potential, and high performance. I've dedicated my life to the pursuit of helping others strategically, radically, and permanently increase their energy, their engagement, and their enthusiasm—*their internal charge*—in every area of life. I've helped executives reinvigorate not just themselves but their entire companies, couples reignite their love lives, athletes get their mojo back, artists reconnect with their higher genius, parents revivify their relationships with their children, and celebrities and politicians reenergize their followerships, all by helping them tap into a stronger internal charge—something they already had waiting within them. For this work, I've become one of the best-paid high-performance coaches and trainers in the world, and my world-renowned seminar, High Performance Academy, sets the standard in the personal growth and effectiveness business. But here's the thing: this isn't about me, and it never has been. I don't do this by chest pounding or by hyping you up with affirmations. I do this by building a strategic plan that allows you—no, that *challenges you*—to live your best life.

Modern Motivations

It's time we all got more strategic and purposeful in how we live our lives.

Why is it that in our abundant world of choice and connectivity so many of us feel lacking and detached? With all the how-to information available at our fingertips, why are we so unsure of which levers to pull to dramatically improve our lives? How is it that we have so much—a roof over our heads, opportunity, safety, choices, access to the entire world—and yet don't feel sparked with energy *all the time* (or at least a lot more of the time)?

In days gone by, self-help gurus and armchair psychologists would respond to these questions by suggesting that we're all crazy, ungrateful, or oblivious of all the good things being heaped upon us. They would say we are driven by dark needs that don't allow us to bask in the sunlight, that we are too trapped in the past, that we expect too much, that we are unconscious of our real thoughts and patterns, or that we are not sending out enough powerful thoughts to attract the happiness in life that we deserve. These answers, of course, are inadequate. In fact, they have caused more harm than good.

So . . . back to the essential question: With so many of our basic human needs now being met, why don't we feel more electrified and satisfied with our lives?

The answer introduces a controversial argument: We feel unsatisfied because the entire baseline of our human motivations has *evolved*. What made us feel happy, energized, and fulfilled just fifty years ago no longer applies, because our brains, bodies, and society have changed so radically.

Such evolutionary language riles a lot of old-school biologists, who argue that the human brain and body could not have evolved fast enough in the past half-century to change our collective human motivations—that as a species, we've always been motivated by the same basic human needs. Even if that's true—and many have argued otherwise—what is clear is that in our abundant modern culture, the *way in which* we activate and feel satisfied by those needs has changed entirely.

Consider this. In the most recent eyeblink of our history, our human experience and our collective culture have transformed in every imaginable way: in what we do (more creative and autonomous work now than task-driven, managed, repetitive work); how we get our food and what we eat (leading to an astonishing evolution in the size of our bodies worldwide); where we call home (the global migration into cities); how we interact (a recently interconnected planet working in offices and organizations rather than fields and factories); what we buy (more nonessential purchases based on aesthetic preferences rather than on functionality or utility); how we spend our time (more at work and yet still more in front of the television and computer); how long we live (longer, but with more health problems than ever—many *because* we live longer); and how we structure our organizations and nations (more democracy and tolerance worldwide—a trend closely tracked since 1981). If you could hopscotch back through history to fifty or a hundred years ago, you would see how much *everything* has changed. And having changed our world so completely, it was inevitable that we humans ourselves should also change in order to survive and thrive. The ways we think, feel, and behave—our psychology—had to keep pace with our world. Thus, the way we express and meet our human drives has evolved.

As our society becomes more abundant, people are no longer driven by just what they *need*. Most of our basic human needs for food, shelter, safety, and belonging have been met and structured by an advancing society. Yet meeting those needs does not, by itself, make us happy. Far from it. Unfortunately, much of our basic understanding of pop psychology still comes from Abraham Maslow's famous "hierarchy of needs" developed in the 1940s. Maslow was brilliant, and much of his work was misinterpreted, but its lasting legacy is this: if we can meet our needs, we should be happy. So when we have our needs met and *don't* feel happy, we all feel that something is wrong with us.

The reality is that in an abundant culture we simply no longer have to focus as much on what we need, so we focus on what we *want*. We have more options and, thus, more freedom to choose what we want our lives to be about. Surrounded by a million choices, we are freed from the constraints of need and yet, at the same time, challenged to find our focus and meaning in life. But no one would suggest that we turn back the clock. It's a blessing to be able to search for what we want. It just so happens that what we want today is very, very different from what we wanted just a decade ago.

Think about how the tidal shift from needs to wants has washed ashore at work. Our modern workforce isn't driven by the mere security of a paycheck or the primitive motivation of the carrot-and-stick wielded by manipulative managements. Today's workers have a new and insatiable hunger for intrinsic motivations, especially the engagement and fulfillment that comes from projects involving creative control, social connectivity, design, story, and contributions that extend beyond the confines of the cubicle and the greater organization. We've become an on-the-go, "friended" workforce that places social interaction, aesthetic experience, innovation, and meaningful collaboration at the top of our priority list when evaluating jobs, causes, projects, and leaders. The old concepts of motivation at work, based solely on compensation, a corner office, and long-term ladder-climbing ambitions, no longer apply (and haven't for a decade). We just aren't as fooled by all the usual trappings of success anymore, because in an already abundant society, *what drives us* has changed. Our modern lives simply don't function based solely on the same considerations of security and sustenance anymore, nor do we see our path to self-actualization the same way we saw it even a generation ago. With all the choice we have, we'll skip traditional security and instead seek novel, challenging, connected, and creative experiences. This isn't just the ramblings of a self-confessed modern free agent. Neuroscience is proving that indeed, when our brains are free from the basic animal needs of safety, what engages the most neural activity are those very things: *novelty, challenge, connection,* and *expression.* And many of the world's largest happiness surveys are finding the same at a global level—we want to feel engaged at work, and what makes us engaged are things like choice, contribution, and creative expression.

We have watched our professional and personal lives blend more and more, until the concept of work/life balance seems a nostalgic pipe dream from the 1950s. Today our home lives are more hectic, stressful, and unstable than they have ever been. People have trouble staying together or even getting along. Parents have a hard time understanding what drives their children's behavior, let alone their own. With the kids booked up doing after-school activities, and Mom and Dad at work all the time, what can families *really* hope to accomplish together? Putting a roof over your family's head, or food on the table, isn't enough anymore, no matter how much you might wish it were. In a hyperconnected and abundant world, your family members are supremely aware of the choices they have. Every day they see better houses, parents, schools, and toys and gadgets on television and the Web. So they care little that they have what they need—that, for them, is a given. They care about having what they *want.*

How can we think more strategically about ourselves and what motivates us today when meeting our basic human needs simply isn't moving the happiness needle out of the blah zone? What's going to lead us to exciting, fulfilling lives amid the sea change going on in our workplaces and our personal lives? How do we get that spark back into our lives, so that what we do fills us with joy and satisfaction? What levers can we pull on this grand ride of life so that we reach our full potential and travel in style to our destiny?

In *The Charge*, I'll answer these questions by proposing a new framework for thinking about human motivation—one that moves us away from merely doing what we need to do to feel secure and comfortable and into the drives that make us feel truly *alive*. Along the way, we'll go deep inside your mind and understand the structure of your brain, and we're going to give you the mental levers to actually *change* that wiring. The mixed bag of emotions that you feel about your life and your work is going to be laid bare before you, and, perhaps for the first time in your conscious adult life, you're going to learn how to control, reassemble, and reconfigure it so that you can experience the Charged Life.

A Charged Life is a consciously designed existence that feels evenly engaged, energized, and enthusiastic. It's a life that is purposefully chosen and activated by leveraging the 10 drives that make us human, which are the subject of this book. The Charged Life is not a one-time feeling or a fleeting spark. It's an enduring flame in the soul that illuminates you throughout all your days no matter the darkness around you. Nor is it about wandering around with a fake perma-grin or feeling supercaffeinated or amped up by some syrupy cocktail of self-help affirmations. It is about elevated yet consistently even energy that is strategically planned for and sustainable, allowing you to be fully engaged in the moment and optimistic about the future. I'll further describe this life in the next chapter, but for now you should underline the operative phrase in its definition: *a consciously designed existence*.

In order to better design your life, you'll need to understand and activate 10 simple drives of human emotion and happiness. These are the psychological levers that you can use to reshape and reenergize your entire life. In section I of this book I'll teach you to understand and leverage what I call your five "baseline drives," which are the most automatic desires you have to develop control, competence, congruence, caring, and connections with others in your life. In section II, I'll unveil the "forward drives," which will help you use change, challenge, creative expression, contribution, and consciousness to radically advance your life. Together, the baseline and forward drives add up to the 10 human drives that will help you ignite your new and fully Charged Life.

All this "change your life" stuff might sound grossly exaggerated and out of reach, if not for some recent advances in the fields of neuroscience, positive psychology, and high performance. We've learned more about how our brains function in the past three years than in the previous three thousand. We've broken psychology's century-old focus on neurosis and what's wrong with us and reframed our study on what's *right* with us. We've cracked the code on what it takes for you to perform at higher levels of joy, engagement, and productivity.

Now is the time to bring our new understanding of human experience to the forefront of how we structure and strategize our lives. The timing couldn't be better. You see the disenchantment, lack of direction, and soul-searching of your family members, friends, neighbors, and office mates. Everybody is looking for something, but he or she isn't sure what it is or where to look for it. The answers, as usual, are already within us. We simply have to understand ourselves better and activate the parts of us that make our lives rich, colorful, connected, and meaningful.

I won't pretend the journey to knowing oneself is an easy one. In consciously deciding to take the reins of your life and ride off in a new direction, you're going to find yourself (at first, anyway) on a bumpy, uncomfortable road. But that's okay—it's the only road worth taking. Life change is hard. Believe me, I know. It's taken car accidents and career changes and chaos and epic internal struggles to get me here, living my best life. But along the way I've learned to direct my human drives better, and because of that I live a life of joy, vibrancy, and fulfillment that I could never have imagined. So have my clients. I want the same for you, and to help you get there, I'm willing to rattle your cage and drive you from the land of comfort (which is also the land of mediocrity). I hope you'll play along, because the alternative—staying on the same path, hoping for something better while refusing to act boldly—is beneath you. Our times are calling for you to master your mind and contribute more magic and positive energy to the world. We all need *you* fully engaged again and sharing with us the fully expressed, extraordinary you. We need you to choose a different kind of life and to charge up for the challenges that lie ahead for all humankind.

When Willpower Trumps Brainpower

No matter your position, circumstances, or opportunities in life, you always have the freedom of mind to choose how you experience, interpret, and, ultimately, shape your world. If you can believe this, then you can strategically choose and create a Charged Life. I believe this now more than ever, and not just at a philosophical level but at a very practical and physical level as well.

Despite being known worldwide as the high-performance guy, I recently lost the charge in life for a period of several months. I had to get incredibly conscious and focused in order to stoke my internal flame and reignite my life. I had to fight, *every single day*, to activate the 10 human drives that are the guts of this book. In the process, I learned that our minds are more powerful than most of us imagine—stronger even than our brains, but we'll get to that.

To be honest, I've lost and reclaimed the charge in my life three times. The first was when I fell into a depression after a terrible breakup with my high school sweetheart in college. I was in a horrible space, suicidal, for an entire year, and it took a car accident to shake me out of it. (I wrote of that accident in my earlier books *The Millionaire Messenger* and *Life's Golden Ticket*.) In brief, after being in a car that flipped over a curve at eighty-five miles an hour, I learned that when we crash onto death's doorstep, we're all forced to ask three questions: *Did I live? Did I love? Did I matter?* It was a soul-shaking experience, to say the least, and it made me question everything in my life. I had never really lived life before, and the accident made me get serious about doing so. It was Virgil's quote that summed up my feelings: "Death twitches my ear. '*Live*,' he says, 'I am coming.' " I decided to use my ticket to a second chance to consciously create a better life, so that when I round my final corner, I'll be happy with the answers at the end.

My ticket turned out to be good for fifteen remarkable years of vibrancy, connection, and meaning. In that span of time, I discovered and mastered the 10 human drives you will learn in this book. I built multimillion-dollar businesses, coached some of the world's most famous celebrities and executives, wrote a few books, fell in love, got married, supported my family in difficult times, traveled the world, blasted easily through almost every challenge, spoke on stages with legendary thought leaders and motivators, hung out with moguls and ex-presidents, and gave and achieved more than I could ever have imagined. I was living the fully Charged Life, and everyone around me always asked, "How in the world do you have so much fun, focus, and energy?"

Then, recently, everything changed. My father, whom I loved dearly and who was my best friend, was diagnosed with and died suddenly of leukemia. As I'll share later, I held it together the best I could for quite some time. I had all the mental levers to cope with our sudden loss, thank God, and fortunately I used them well enough to stay strong for him, myself, and my family during that difficult time. Still, there is no doubt my charge deminished with the sudden loss of Dad.

Then, more recently, things completely fell apart in an instant—in another accident. Ironically, the third time I lost the charge happened just as I began to write this book.

I remember the day vividly. A group of close friends and I were racing down a deserted white-sand beach in Mexico on ATVs. The sky was a perfect cool blue, the air just slightly humid. The ocean was smooth and calm, the color of turquoise. I had been riding through the desert all day, smartly and safely. Heading down one of the final stretches of beach, I was relaxed, breathing in deeply, enjoying the adrenaline from a good ride and the blessings of a picture-perfect setting. That day, I was thinking a lot of my dad. He had taught me to ride, to live.

Maybe there was a moment when I lost my presence, tuning out for just a moment and gazing out at the ocean for just a beat too long. Whatever the case, cruising down the beach at thirty-five miles an hour, I didn't see the little pillow of sand in front of me. Unlike the slow-motion special effects when our car flipped into the air and off the highway fifteen years earlier, this time everything happened *fast*. The ATV hit the pillow of sand, went airborne, and landed on the front left tire in such a way that it flipped hard to the left, slamming me onto the ground. I felt the impact of the sand and the air bursting out of my lungs. I remember rolling along the ground and the scratching sound of sand beating against my helmet. I could hear the ATV bouncing alongside me—boom! boom! boom!—and I thought, *God, please don't let that thing land on me.*

I awoke to my friends huddled and kneeling around me, and asking if I was okay. The guide just kept repeating, "Did it land on you? Did it land on you? Did it land on you?" I didn't know and couldn't reply. I was blinking the stars away from my vision, trying to catch my breath. Closing my eyes, I tried to feel my body, and it took a few seconds to sense anything at all. My head hurt; my left leg was numb; my left arm was screaming. The guide started patting down my body, looking for any bones sticking out or internal swelling around my ribs and stomach. My friends helped me sit up, and I blacked out briefly, just for a second. That's when I knew I was in trouble. My entire left side hurt fiercely: head, shoulder, wrist, ribs, hip.

My friends deserve a medal for getting me onto the back of an ATV, then getting me to base camp and then into town to the hospital—a two-hour window of time that was more brutal than I care to remember. The initial verdict wasn't so bad: a broken wrist, which required surgery, a few bruised ribs that wouldn't let me breathe normally for a couple of weeks, a wicked case of whiplash, and a very sore hip and shoulder. I thought I got off lucky.

Three months later, though, right when I started writing this book, my life was a mess. I couldn't concentrate. I was having trouble planning, imagining, remembering things. My mental speed of judgment was sluggish, and my hand-eye coordination seemed lacking in racquetball. Successes were feeling hollow, and I seemed unable to resonate or empathize well with people. My mood was all over the place, and I was acting impulsively. I didn't feel alert, engaged, connected, or satisfied in any way. Worse, I wasn't coping well anymore—sad thoughts about my father's death were consuming me. The charge was *gone.*

Feeling adrift in the random flow of life, I was unhappy and unfulfilled. Like a lot of people, I just pushed aside my reality, blaming my emotional malaise and erratic behavior on busyness. *I must just be tired and stressed*, I thought, *but this too shall pass if I just keep on keeping on.* After all, I had all I was supposed to have to be happy: gorgeous wife, loving family, passionate work, cool cars, nice houses, celebrities on speed dial. But something was very much amiss.

It turned out that writing this book saved my life. I'd been researching neuroscience for years to clarify and support my beliefs about what drives human behavior and motivation. I had learned a lot about the brain, and one morning something happened that made me think of my neuroscience research.

After weeks of battling with writing issues, one evening I had a caffeine-fueled breakthrough and wrote twenty pages. The next morning, I ran to the computer and started scanning what I had written the night before. It's weird how just a few moments can change your life forever. Right there on the screen, I discovered that I needed help. What I saw was sentence after sentence with missing words. Somehow, the words I was thinking weren't coming out through my fingertips to the keyboard. Worse, in many of the sentences, I couldn't even decipher my own meaning well enough to fill in the gaps. In reading what I had written, I was terrified to see an illogical soup of fragmentary thoughts and sentences. Something was clearly wrong with my language skills and memory.

All this sparked concern and reminded me of what I had been researching in neuroscience—specifically, how people with brain injuries often have language issues. But they also tend to have issues with vision, impulse control, empathy, memory, and motor control. I hadn't had *all* those issues, too, since my accident . . . had I?

Suddenly, I realized that there wasn't something wrong with "me"—there was something wrong with *my brain*. Moments from the past few months came to mind: that time when I was shooting a video for my customers and my right eye started wandering suddenly, out of sync with my left; that time I decided, quite out of the blue, to buy a car (not exactly a decision to be impulsive on, which my wife was quick to point out); those times I didn't feel joy or connection when I usually did; the troubles I was having paying attention on important projects; the sudden inability to cope with strong emotions, like the sadness of losing my dad; how my team kept asking me if there was "something wrong," because they didn't feel my usual presence or empathetic resonance. The list went on.

Within days, I had a brain scan, and the final verdict from my acccident was in: I had a form of brain trauma—postconcussive syndrome—with low activity in the prefrontal cortex, cerebellum, and hippocampus. I took a few cognitive tests that further confirmed the verdict. My cognitive ability was in the lower 25th percentile of high school graduates. The damage to my prefrontal cortex was undermining my concentration, emotional control, and abstract reasoning abilities; the low activity in my cerebellum was slowing my ability to make decisions; and my poorly functioning hippocampus gave me a really bad memory—all major problems when you're navigating life, let alone taking a cognitive test or writing a book.

Fortunately, the human brain is often repairable. Just as you rehab any other part of your injured body, you can rehab your brain by focused and consistent practice and therapy. Leveraging the brain's capacity for what neuroscientists call "neuroplasticity," you can aim your thoughts and experiences in a way that reshapes and restrengthens the damaged parts of your brain. Specifically, by taking on new challenges and using conscious thought, meditation, and mind puzzles to activate low-performing parts of your brain, you can, as my friend and leading neuroscientist Dr. Daniel Amen says, "change your brain and change your life."

As I wrote these pages, I had to struggle with all my might to get back the charge. I had to practice mind over matter, using my thoughts and attention to reactivate parts of my brain and reenergize my life. I had to put into practice everything I've ever learned in psychology, neuroscience, and high performance. I fought every single day to find the raw willpower needed to focus my attention, muster my energies, overcome my physical limitations, and bang on these keys for you. I spilled my blood on these pages, testing the boundaries of my own philosophies.

I've been with people as they coped with major illness, injuries, and death. My accident, my story, wasn't all that dramatic or earthshaking in the big picture. I share it because I've fought through the challenges, learning to consciously control my mind and my life, which is exactly what I'll be asking you to do. I did this under extreme emotional stress, with limited mental focus and capacity, at a time when I had enormous expectations on me to write this book and run a multimillion-dollar business. I was traveling all the time while I was trying to care for my wife and family, my friends, my team, my customers, and myself. The one thing that kept it all together was that I had a plan. I knew the path back to a vibrant life. I knew the 10 drives of human experience and happiness. All I had to do was work my butt off to activate them.

I'm happy to report I'm *back*, fully restored, fully charged. I cannot possibly describe the levels of energy, engagement, and enthusiasm I have in life again, thanks to the most disciplined efforts I've ever given to activating the strategies in this book. Instead of describing the feeling, I'll let you discover it for yourself in the pages ahead.

What I will share with you now is that I'm simply thankful that I knew which levers to push and pull in my life to ensure that I didn't slip into pools of sadness or apathy during one of the hardest times of my life. Writing about the Charged Life and the 10 human drives reminded me how much control I had over my life, no matter how broken it was. And it kept me focused on what mattered as I struggled toward what became a full and healthy recovery. My greatest ambition is that it does the same for you. Personally, I think your life is on the line every single day you exist. Your ultimate life experience and legacy is being built moment by moment, day by day. Your story is being crafted by your every action, all leading somewhere, all leading to what one hopes will be a magnificent crescendo. Perhaps you don't need a whack on the head like I did to decide to fight and struggle for a better quality of life. Perhaps you'll just choose, in this very second, to activate the best within you once more.

This is your time. Your destiny awaits. Ready yourself. Let's roll.

Chapter One

OUT OF
THE DARKNESS

Over the past fifteen years as a high-performance student and coach, I've been blessed to see the dramatic transformations people can make in their day-to-day lives when they simply *choose* to climb out of the half-lit mediocrity of an unengaged and unfulfilling existence. I've also seen people with already happy lives amplify their joy and satisfaction to levels they had yet to imagine. Regardless of where you are in that spectrum, it helps to know just what kind of life you're in, and the type of person you are that led you to that life, sooner than later. With that in mind we begin with an exploration of three very different kind of lives.

Three Lives

A Charged Life is a very different kind of life from the one most people lead. That's not because it's unattainable, but rather because most people rarely think about (or strategically manage) their long-term energy and engagement in life—what we'll call their "charge level." They don't think of their lives this way, because most are simply trying to muster up enough energy to get through their busy, exhausting days. They're puttering along from one week to the next, just trying to make it to the weekend, when they can collapse on the couch or do something they really want to do. What they don't often understand is that the *busyness* of our lives has a funny way of creating a myopic vision of what's real or possible. When you can't see past your own day planner, it's hard to see the cumulative reality of who you have become and where you are headed.

Sometimes it's helpful just to stop amid all our craziness, poke our heads above our busywork and computer screens, and ask ourselves about the overall feel and quality of our lives. We should gauge our own charge levels, asking just how excited we really feel about our current reality and our future.

Feeling charged means feeling *engaged*, *energetic*, and *enthusiastic*, and I'm pretty sure everybody wants that. Our charge levels have two properties: quality and intensity. The quality of the emotional charge we have in life can be positive or negative, and it can also be low-intensity (barely humming) or high-intensity (cranking at full volume). So, ideally, we all would have a desirably intense and positive charge in life. But do *you* have it? Is the quality and intensity of the charge you currently feel every day what you had always hoped to experience in life? Does the charge you're giving at work have the quality and intensity that inspires you and others? Does the charge you're giving to your spouse, to your kids, have the quality and intensity that effectively communicates your adoration and affection for them?

After fifteen years of studying the human condition, I've come to see that people tend to live one of three types of life. You have one of these lives today, and you can choose to keep it, amplify it, or change it altogether. Let's take a tour through all three types so that we can better differentiate the Charged Life from others and then go about the business of strategically creating it.

The Caged Life

Many people live their lives caged either in the past or in the expectations of others. They have never really ventured into the unknown or sought to break the boundaries that they or others have set for them. Because they have let other people or the past dictate who they are, their identities are trapped in a tight box of beliefs about what is possible for them. Thus, their experience in life and their everyday thoughts, feelings, and behaviors are restricted. They generally feel tethered to where they are, bound by experiences they never got over, ruled by the results of yesterday, scared to disappoint their masters—masters that may well exist only in their minds. They often feel that the world has cornered them into a certain way of being and won't let them escape, lashing them to false or unfair labels, expectations, and assumptions.

From birth, we are enticed with carrots-and-sticks to do what others want us to do. Our "handlers," or caregivers, wanted us to display a certain look or identity to the world. Sometimes, they coaxed us into behaving as they wanted, by offering us treats of acceptance and love. Other times, they may have been more heavy-handed. The end result, inevitably, was that we adapted our behaviors and our desires to fall in line with external rewards. After a time, it became easy to accept this reality as routine. As long as we were receiving attention, care, and rewards, being in the cage had a lot going for it.

Moriah, a one-time client of mine, felt that way—trapped by a desire to gain the approval and love of others. When I started coaching her, she was always complaining, *"No one understands me or gives me a chance—I'm just a prisoner of what everyone else wants and thinks of me."* Despite this complaint, she never stuck her neck out and expressed who she was or what she herself wanted in life. She had gone to a school her parents wanted her to attend, she took a job her friends thought would be good for her, and she moved to a city her boyfriend always wanted to live in (which she secretly hated).

She moved, spoke, and acted like she thought others wanted her to, and she never ventured far from her routines because she feared failing and being judged by others. Her entire existence was a projection of others' wishes, and she was never strong enough to look in the mirror and ask what she really wanted.

This is the imprisoned, obedient life. At some point, we all have felt its stultifying repression. We felt locked in, controlled, restless to get out. Not all of us have broken free, and here's the really sobering part: some never will.

There are only two ways out of the cage. The first happens when, by chance or fate, life flips it upside down, smashing our cozy reality and breaking open the cage for good. The second way out, the willful way, takes a massive personal effort. It happens when we finally choose to look beyond the bars of our approval- and fear-driven experience and see that there is more to life than being squeezed into someone else's cage. It happens when we do the one thing that has ever helped anyone design a different destiny: consciously choose a new self-image and life, and fight to forge it into existence by consistently aligning our thoughts and behaviors to make it so.

The Comfortable Life

For many of us, life is not as dire as the caged life. Through work, dedication, and fortunate circumstances, many of us live what I think of as the comfortable life. We've followed similar paths to independence, opportunity, and freedom. We have houses, spouses, cars, and kids. We feel engaged and thankful for our lives. We know we've made some trade-offs—a little less adventure here, a few more hours at the office there—but we knew what we were getting ourselves into. We saw our friends and peers take a similar journey, and they seemed happy.

And then one day, someone asks about your life, and you're surprised to hear yourself reply, "Oh, things are . . . you know . . . fine."

Trouble begins to brew in the back of your mind: *Is this what I really wanted? Is this all there is? Have I made too many trade-offs? Am I living my life or someone else's? Aren't I more creative and sexy and spontaneous and ambitious and fun than this?*

Often, your brain responds to this kind of thinking with the sharp tool of guilt: *You don't know how good you've got it. You should feel so much more grateful. Can't you just be satisfied with what you have?*

Though more of a rut than a cage, we start to feel trapped. Make no mistake: the trappings are much, much more comfortable, and the door to possibility is much bigger and more accessible—a free-swinging gateway to more, more, more. But even in the comfort comes a restless stirring.

Life feels not meaningless but mysterious. You wonder, *How did I end up here? Where did my ambition and drive and excitement go?*

While the caged self comes to see the world as scary, the comfortable self sees it as stale. The caged self feels it has no potential; the comfortable self has actively sought to realize its potential but fears it has peaked. The caged self feels limited by external conditions; the comfortable self feels limited by its own success. The caged self feels it has no voice and, thus, doesn't use it; the comfortable self has used its voice, shared it, banked on it . . . but now wonders if that voice is the right one, the authentic one.

There is, however, one undeniable similarity between the caged and the comfortable: whether caught in a cage or in the trappings of success, both desire more color, variety, creativity, freedom, and connection. Both long for the Charged Life.

The Charged Life

The one living a caged life asks, *Will I survive?* So the focus is always on whether the person will be safe or be hurt. The one living a comfortable life asks, *Will I be accepted and succeed?* So he or she focuses on belonging and satiation. The person living a Charged Life wonders, *Am I living my truth and actualizing my potential? Am I living an inspired life and inspiring others?* The boredom, or aimlessness, that the comfortable self feels isn't in the emotional repertoire of someone with a Charged Life, because of the joy and purpose the charged feels in engaging in new and challenging activities. While the comfortable self feels that life is mysterious, the charged self finds life magical and meaningful. The comfortable self sees the world as familiar and therefore stale; the charged self sees the same world filled with exciting and unlimited possibilities for growth and progress.

We who live fully charged don't feel disengaged or restless because of the trappings of our lives. We are not passengers on the collective march of progress—we're creating our own world and our own definitions of what it means to live and progress. We are fully living and experiencing the lives we want, not coveting or chasing others' lives.

We haven't been on cruise control in years; we experience the zest of fully conscious control and presence, fine-tuning the pressure on the gas pedal for ourselves in every moment, whether we choose to roar ahead or slow down to enjoy the scenery.

We are not trapped in the ruts of routine or old, familiar skill sets; rather, we are engaged in the present. Unlike the comfortable, we *want and hunger* for the challenges that stretch our abilities. We don't question our merits or doubt our strengths; rather, we focus on a lofty ambition to contribute to the world, and we call forth all our energies to do so.

When we live the Charged Life, we don't worry about making waves; we worry about doing what's right and what's meaningful. If controversy or hurt feelings happen along the way, we meet them with our full presence and care—but we march on.

At first glance, it would seem that those living the Charged Life have surpassed all obstacles and are living a charmed existence. But that's not exactly right. It's just that those with high charge levels *enjoy* the journey they're on no matter what obstacles present themselves; they are deeply *enthusiastic* about facing life's challenges and designing their own destinies. They know they are works in progress, but they take pleasure in shaping themselves and reinventing their realities. In this way, unlike the caged or the comfortable, they are not asking reality or life to make them safe or satiated at all. Instead, they look forward to the opportunities for change and growth. They focus on serving and contributing to the world. Their credo is: *ask not what you are getting from the world but, rather, what you are giving to the world.*

To the caged or the comfortable, the Charged Life seems like an unattainable star in the sky, a fiery energy and light in its own orbit. Indeed, the Charged Life seems to fly above the fray, fueled by an entirely different energy and bound for an entirely different destination. Yet those living the Charged Life are quite grounded, and many will tell you they themselves were once either caged or comfortable, or even both. For it is often the human condition to comply obediently at first, then to assert but still cooperate or compromise, then, finally, to discover choice, calling, maturity, and heightened drives for freedom, expression, and contribution. The Charged Life, then, usually calls to us after we have done what we were supposed to do, become who we thought we were supposed to be, lived as we thought we were supposed to live. Then the safety and comfort and compromise get to us, and a stirring of restlessness and revolution sends us off in search of greater adventures and meaning.

When we find it, the Charged Life feels unlike anything we have ever known. It has an even energy of enthusiasm about it that seems to endure no matter the circumstances or challenges we face.

Meet the Chargers

When you discover yourself living a Charged Life, you notice an even, confident, buoyant, and sustained energy about yourself. You have high energy, complete engagement in your endeavors, and a palpable enthusiasm about your life and future.

Some people suggest that not everyone can have this kind of life. But why not? "Chargers," the name I give to those living a Charged Life, are not born with some kind of lighthing bolt on their heads. They are not different from anyone else, you or me. If there is a difference, it's that they act and perceive the world and themselves *differently*. Few of them blame their childhoods for their adult choices or challenges. They don't harbor a lot of resentment or attachment to the past. They don't seem to be distracted in the present. And they don't fear the future or the inevitable obstacles that life throws at them. In this way, they indeed seem different from others.

But it's not the lack of attachment to fear or the negative aspects of life that make Chargers so fascinating and empowered. Rather, it's their ability to exude a grounded, positive, and even energy, engagement, and enthusiasm in life regardless of the situation they find themselves in. This isn't always easy. One thing I hear over and over from those living a Charged Life is how *consistently* they practice being conscious of their reactions and realities. They *work* for their charges, and they know they have to. Chargers don't think their internal charges are a gifted or "set" mind-set, or a permanent personality. (And they're right: neuroscientists have written that the adult brain and personality are not "set" but rather continue to grow and mature based on new ideas, experiences, and conditioning. This is hopeful news for anyone who believes his brain or personality prevents him from having a Charged Life.) Chargers, it turns out, are incredibly attentive to their internal and external realities, and they work hard to have the traits everyone might assume they readily have.

Here are the seven most common attributes of Chargers that I've discovered:

1. Chargers are open and observant in the moment.

Informed about but not confined by the past, Chargers are aware and accepting of the present moment. They tend to engage with great curiosity, spontaneity, and flexibility in the world unfolding around them. They do not rush to judge what things mean or bind themselves closely with an assumption of how things "should" turn out. With this full palette of perception, they tend to be more patient, more tolerant, more receptive of whatever comes their way, and more creative in how they understand a situation. They feel that the journey is just as important as the destination, so they seek to immerse themselves, fully engaged, in the now.

2. Chargers are future oriented.

For all their ability to be present in the moment, Chargers also have grand visions and ambitions. They have richly detailed visions of the future and actively seek to make those visions realities. Chargers are optimistic about the future, and that optimism works like a magnet, drawing that desired future to them. They are genuinely enthusiastic about their envisioned futures and feel empowered to take the steps necessary to turn their dreams into realities. They see problems in the present as solvable, and so they endeavor to solve them and make the future world a better place.

3. Chargers are challenge seekers.

Much of the excitement for life that Chargers experience comes from their active pursuit of novel challenges. As you will learn in the coming chapters, novel challenge is like brain candy, activating the pleasure centers and hormones of the brain. Those with Charged Lives want to stretch, express, and realize themselves, and they know that this cannot come about without challenge. Chargers are ready for whatever life throws at them because they believe that they can rise to the demands of any situation. This allows them to enjoy and even be playful amid the uncertain, tumultuous process of growth.

4. Chargers are deeply interested in, and authentically connect with, others.

Simply put, Chargers *love* people. They have a deep sense of curiosity and respect for others. They ask a lot of questions and genuinely listen to the dreams, fears, and daily realities of others.

They are not merely social butterflies, breezy in their interactions with others. Quite the contrary, they tend to focus intently on others, and they have authentic interactions with people and deep, meaningful relationships with their friends and families. While they are generally seen as more outgoing or extroverted than other people, they are thoughtful conversationalists and have few superficial relationships. They see each relationship in life as an opportunity for connecting, learning, growing, and sharing a piece of themselves. Chargers say the relationships they have with others are often the most important things in their lives; relationships are seen as the key vehicle to engaging in and enjoying life.

5. Chargers are self-reliant.

Despite their drive to connect with others, Chargers are extremely independent and resourceful. They march to their own drummers; they welcome company on their journeys, but not to the extent that they are willing to divert their paths. They do not feel responsible for making everyone around them happy if it means compromising their own values. For this, they're often seen unfairly as stubborn or self-minded mavericks. But the reality is that they are simply brave enough to chart their own courses and confident enough on their journeys to try new ideas, and even to fail and figure things out for themselves.

6. Chargers are creatively driven.

Creative expression is a big part of Chargers' lives. They tend to choose jobs, careers, projects, causes, and opportunities based on whether they feel they can be creative and expressive. Thus, in any given situation, Chargers tend to be the creators, artists, designers, storytellers, and thought leaders. They actively engage their creative sides and tune in to their own unique expressive perspectives. Thus, their expressive talents tend to make them stand out. They also tend to be unapologetic for their styles or perspectives, instead taking pride in their boldness and their commitment to sharing their works.

7. Chargers are meaning makers.

Chargers have a deep respect for the meaning that imbues each day and an equally deep desire to create meaningful moments in their lives. By looking for significant meaning in their lives, Chargers are able to avoid getting bogged down in the details that tend to draw other people up short. Chargers have a full appreciation for the "big picture"; their lives are spent striving to achieve worthy goals that tie to their passions and lives' purposes. They know, as Viktor

Frankl taught us, that man's real search is for a meaningful existence. Through this understanding, Chargers have a high facility for consciously determining what things mean, with a tendency to positively interpret both their struggles and successes in life. Chargers also try to create meaningful moments and memories with others, often surprising others with gifts, unique experiences, or simply kind words of love, admiration, or appreciation.

Reading these descriptions of Chargers might make it seem as if Chargers had some unique gift or were "always this way." But, again, those living Charged Lives will often tell you they once had caged or comfortable lives. The transformation in their lives happened when they *decided* to transform themselves. They felt a desire to have more *life in their lives*, and then they worked toward achieving that desire. In the same way, you, too, can become more fully charged in life— by your own conscious choice and consistent action. But how shall you begin?

The 10 Human Drives

If you were to consciously design your ideal life, what should you pay attention to, and what levers could you pull to consistently improve your life and sustain higher levels of energy, engagement, and enthusiasm?

Think about that for a moment. In the best moments of your life, there was a spark. You felt it, and you never completely forgot it. So the question is, what drove that spark? What was it that made you feel so alive? And how do you bring that feeling into your everyday life? Better yet, how do you turn that spark into a lasting flame and fire in the soul—a charge within yourself that never goes out?

The answers to these questions don't involve quick fixes or superficial approaches that give you a quick boost. An energy drink could do that for you, but you already know that doesn't last. Creating a Charged Life requires us to dig deep inside and activate the very drives that make us human.

My research and practice have always sought to understand how to activate those drives in ways that cause real, lasting change and engagement in today's chaotic world. I created the 10 Human Drives framework, and I've had tremendous success teaching others to use it to radically and strategically change their lives. Further, I showed them how to use these human drives in today's context—to activate the basic drives we've all felt as humans over the past fifty years or so—in ways that make them feel happy and energized in this changed, abundant society.

Before we jump in, though, let me clarify what I mean by "human drives." I think of our human drives as psychological motivators tied more to wants than to needs. We don't necessarily *need* to have or meet any of the elements in my model. In the twentieth century, a set of psychological theories referred to as "drive theories" advanced the idea that we all were born with certain physical needs and that if we didn't satisfy those needs as soon as possible, we would experience adverse states of tension and negative emotion. When I use the word "drive," I don't think of it as a physical or psychological *need* at all. In fact, outside of a very limited set of life-sustaining needs— food, water, sleep, protection from the elements, care at birth—I don't believe we have any more real *needs*. Some people see personal growth or "actualization" as a human need, but then, how do you explain your neighbor's thirty-five-year-old son who won't leave the couch and stretch himself in the world? Other popular states and traits, such as morality, love, self-esteem, respect, faith, and transcendence, are also not real needs. Strong, important, and life-enhancing desires? Yes. But matters of life and death? Not for most.

Consider one of the first human drives, the drive for control.

Naturally, we are all driven to have more control in our lives because we believe that more control can lead to greater happiness. But if we don't have more control, we certainly don't flip out and lose our ability to engage, function, or be productive. Creative expression—yet another drive I'll propose in this framework—is something we all want, too, though many can and do live without it. Yes, without it we are not *as* happy, but we can still get by. Control and creative expression are really things we *want*, not things we need in order to live. The same goes for all the drives I'm talking about—we are driven by them because they can and do lead to a better existence, but we don't necessarily *need* them.

Why all the semantic brouhaha here? Because I want to be up front and candid from the outset. You *are* driven by the 10 drives I'm proposing, but you really don't *need* any of these concepts—or my model or even this book—to be happy. There's no question that you can go right on about your life without more control and creative expression.

You could, after all, in this very instant, choose to be happy without having any *more* of anything. If you chose, right now, you could simply close your eyes and bliss out in a state of nirvana. That's the power of the human mind. There's just one problem: it won't last.

It's my belief that the 10 Human Drives are what you really want in life, and if you'll work toward activating them, your efforts will lead to a state of heightened energy, engagement, and enthusiasm—yes, happiness—that will simply astound you.

In section I of this book, I'll cover the first five drives of human motivation, what I call the "baseline drives"—control, competence, congruence, caring, and connection. These are the core drives that contribute to our stability in our sense of self and social belonging.

If we can get all these baseline drives activated and amped up more consistently, we find ourselves suddenly feeling more secure and socially connected. That's a pretty good recipe for happiness, but it's not enough. Activating the first five drives is somewhat akin to meeting our basic needs in a modern society: it's a starting point, but it's not completely satisfying. That's why I call them baseline drives—we gotta have 'em, but all they do is get us in the game. The home runs come in the next five drives, which I call the forward drives—change, challenge, creative expression, contribution, and consciousness. In section II, I'll cover these forward drives, and you'll discover why they often move the needle the most in raising your levels of happiness in life. Though the forward drives are higher-order drives than the first five, all 10 are really vital and important. Can you imagine not activating one of these drives well in your life? Remove any one of them, and your happiness equation in life falls to pieces. Understanding and mastering all 10 human drives seems daunting, but the good news is, you can read this book over and over again until you do.

The chapters ahead, each of which breaks down one of the 10 human drives, are all written with action in mind. I cover a lot of territory on how you should think about each drive, but in the end I propose just three specific strategies you can use to dramatically move the needle in activating each drive. Ten human drives, three needle-moving strategies each, thirty strategies in total. And you don't have to use them all at once. You might simply select one at a time to focus on and see how it affects your life.

In ending this and each chapter ahead, I'd like to encourage you to engage in a series of sentence-completion activities called Charge Points. These are thought-provoking takeaways for you to answer on your own time after thinking about the concepts in each chapter. I'll begin the sentences, and you finish them. I recommend writing these sentences in a personal journal as you go through the book. It will help you reflect on and integrate the lessons.

CHARGE POINTS

1. If I've felt caged or too comfortable in my recent life, it's probably because . . .

2. If I'm going to start experiencing a more Charged Life, I would have to . . .

3. Of all the traits of Chargers—open and observant in the moment, future oriented, challenge seeker, deeply interested in others, self-reliant, creatively driven, meaning maker—the one I could better integrate or amplify in my life would be . . .

THE FIVE
BASELINE DRIVES

CONTROL

COMPETENCE

CONGRUENCE

CARING

CONNECTION

Chapter Two

THE DRIVE FOR
CONTROL

The stability we cannot find in the world, we must create within our own persons.
—Nathaniel Branden

My father, Mel Burchard, was diagnosed with acute myeloid leukemia on Mother's Day, May 10, 2009. It was out of the blue. The week before, he was golfing and playing racquetball. The doctors gave him a 5 percent chance of making it. Both doctors said it was the worst case they had seen in their careers.

Dad was an extraordinary man: funny, supportive, strong, loving. His message to us kids throughout life said everything you needed to know about the man: "Be yourself. Be honest. Do your best. Be a good citizen. Treat people with respect. Follow your dreams."

His dedication to others spoke for itself, too. Twenty years in the Marines, with three tours in Vietnam; twenty years with the State of Montana; thirty-four years with Mom; sixty-nine years as a fine man.

The day after Father's Day, we learned that his second course of chemotherapy was ineffective. The cancer had taken his body. He understood the outcome, and he was at peace with it. He would have only a few weeks to live. Dad chose to be at home, in hospice care, surrounded and cared for by his family.

All the nurses cried when he left the hospital because they all had come to love his humor and his stories about life. Everywhere he went, he respected others and shared a good joke and a story. He set roots of friendship everywhere. Everyone loved him.

In his short time at home, Dad left nothing unsaid and nothing undone. Our immediate family was there: Mom; my two brothers, Bryan and David; my sister, Helen; her husband, Adam; and my wife, Denise.

We were blessed to have this time with him. We got to tell him how proud we were of him, that he had lived a good life, that Mom would always be taken care of, that his values and spirit would live on in each of us. These things were important to him. Until he lost his ability to speak in the final two days, he always asked that we take care of Mom. We will.

It's hard to see your dad fade away. To me, it was the worst thing to ever happen in my entire lifetime, and I hated that I couldn't help it or control it. But Dad faced it with grace and strength, even as the side effects of chemo made him terribly sick. He was appreciative and loving as we cared for him. He knew his time was short, and it was amazing to see him so loving with us, so at peace with what must be.

Dad died just before midnight. By 12:30 a.m. on July 9 the nurse gave the official pronouncement. He went peacefully, without pain, with just a long series of labored breaths spread further and further apart until he was gone. Dad died as I held his right hand, my brother Bryan held his left, and Mom and my sister were by his side. At home with family all around him—exactly as he would have wanted.

A few weekends before Dad died, when we had discovered that his chemotherapy hadn't done the job, I was teaching a seminar. Around four hundred people had traveled from all over the world to attend. I was in San Francisco; Dad was in Nevada, where he and Mom had a second home and where he fell ill. The night before my event, Dad called me and broke the news: he had just a few weeks, they said. He didn't want me to overreact and cancel the seminar—something he knew I would quickly do to go be with him.

The next evening, after teaching for nine hours onstage, I picked up the phone and called Dad. We had come up with the idea of my interviewing him, asking a wide range of questions about his life and recording the conversation to share with my family later. I especially loved one particular message he shared for all of us kids: "Always love your mother and your brothers and sisters, keep faith in yourself, and help other people who are less fortunate than you guys are, and don't be afraid to ask for help and love. Just be good Samaritans and do the best you can."

From that conversation, I learned so much about him. There was no surprising revelation about his life; it was just how he spoke and how he dealt with it all. He had such an openness and optimism about him, a willingness to meet the uncontrollable with a measure of choice and will.

Dad fought the good fight against cancer. During his last week, when it was clear that he would not live to see another, he accepted it and seemed to release any fears. He never complained about anything—not about the pain, not about the bedpans or the constant nosebleeds or the injections or the rolling over to change the sheets. He simply accepted and chose to meet life's biggest and—for most—scariest transition with love and grace. In an uncontrollable situation, he still directed the strength of his character, the Marine in him defining the meaning of it all on his own terms until the very end.

It's not easy to write something like this, trying to keep it short yet express what a remarkable man this was, trying to share an insight with you about control, about life.

To say that death is generally unwelcome and uncontrollable is an understatement. But it happens nonetheless, as do many things we do not plan or wish for. Yet amid all our struggles, even our final battles, should our wits and will allow, we have the ability to control the way we meet the world, define the meaning of our experience, and leave an example of how remarkable we can be throughout it all.

. . .

It would seem odd to begin a book on motivation with a story of death. But I want you to know me, and I want to begin by being truthful—we cannot control everything in our lives. Nor should we attempt to. In fact, I often argue that most of the misery people feel in life comes from attempting to control things that either can't be controlled or are inconsequential. You can't control the weather or the economy. You can't control others—you've learned that by now I'm sure. For the most part, we can control only the quality of our character, actions, and contributions to the world.

Still, the human drive for control runs deep, and we all tend to strive for more of it, until at last it is ultimately taken away from us. In the space in between, we ought to learn the factors we *can* control that make our journeys remarkable. This chapter aims to help you do that.

We start with a quiz:

How in control of your life do you feel today, on a scale of one to ten, with ten representing being in total control?

How in control of your mind, emotions, and experiences do you feel?

How in control are you of the immediate world around you?

Your answers say a lot about how you've chosen to exert yourself in the world, and they correlate directly to your degree of happiness.

Few would argue that we spend much of our lives trying to gain more control, but what, specifically, is it that we're trying to control?

What factors make us feel as though we have enough control to be sane and happy?

Broadly speaking, what we all are after is a sense of control over our inner and outer worlds. We want to have control over our conscious experiences, our thoughts, feelings, and behaviors; we want to control the results we get and the relationships we have in the outside world. *This desire to regulate and influence our overall life experience is what the human drive for control is all about.*

As with all human drives, the drive for control can be a two-edged sword. If we seek too much control, we end up becoming inflexible and rigid. We start expecting everything to turn out exactly according to plan and then lose our ability to be receptive and adaptive to anything we did not anticipate. We try to suppress any variability in our lives, caging ourselves into obsessively controlled routines, relationships, and environments. We collaborate less easily with others, and we tend to treat people harshly when they don't fall in line with what we want. It's terribly restricting and, ultimately, prevents us from experiencing the diversity, color, and joy of a more flexible and released life.

On the flip side, if we have no control in our lives, life can feel like a terrifying tailspin. While relinquishing control for a "going with the flow" attitude may sound wonderful now, it also requires disengaging from what is real. Releasing all control may work at the spa or on a mountaintop, but in life's tumultuous rivers it's generally a bad idea. No control means no choice, no exertion of will, and can leave us helpless. Without exerting control, we can't direct our minds or influence our environment. We are left without the freedom to choose our paths if we leave ourselves completely up to the whims of chance and circumstance.

My aim in discussing each of these drives isn't to tell you how much you should strive either to rein in or cut loose with them. What makes me feel like I'm appropriately in control of my life might be someone else's definition of too much or too little. We all need different levels of control at different points in our lives. While I believe that most of us want to be somewhere in the harmonious middle path between the two extremes of each drive, that's not always the case.

I've found that there are three specific activators that light up our drive for control in a way that makes us feel particularly energized, engaged, and enthusiastic. No matter how much or how little control you prefer, if you're going to control something in life, then the following three areas are what you should direct your attention to.

Activator #1: Control Your Outlook and Character

Most of the events and experiences that happen to you in life are often random, unexpected, coincidental, or, if you prefer, fated—they just happen and are outside of your anticipation. However, your ultimate response—the meaning you give to these occurrences—is 100 percent within your control. In that ability lies the greatest differentiator of human experience and your strongest tool in forging a Charged Life. It turns out that the grandest needle mover in your depth of control over your life is your outlook, the quality of the meaning you attach to the events in your life and your future.

If this is true, it places you in a critical role in life—to serve as guardian to and director of your outlook toward yourself, others, and the world. This is a tougher task than you might imagine, as what you see in the world on a regular basis is what you tend to expect, and what most people are seeing isn't all that positive. Almost everything we see and read today is an advertisement in some form or other for chaos, stress, conflict, negativity, consumerism, or other people's agendas. Consider our modern media-driven world, which seemingly conspires to darken our perspective on humanity. The average American watches four hours of television, most of which merely perpetuates polarization, violence, narcissism, and greed. Worse, we spend another few hours browsing websites that don't add anything to our lives but instead add more distraction and dead ends. If we're spending more than four hours a day seeing and experiencing such things, what shall we begin to expect in the world? Positive things or negative things?

This leads to the obvious: if you're going to maintain a sane and positive perspective about the world, it's important to better guard the information you consume. In all cases, it wouldn't hurt you to *dramatically* decrease your time spent watching television, listening to trash talk radio, surfing the net, or reading celebrity gossip magazines. All that information you are consuming consciously and unconsciously is creating undue stress and unease in your life, and to a degree you probably don't understand. Despite the popular metaphor, your brain is not a computer. Computers don't have emotions; you do. For every bit of data that comes into your life, your brain attaches meaning and emotion to it. This means that information is actually quite "heavy," and the more information coming into your life, the more weight is loading you down. If a computer gets overloaded with too much data, it simply slows down its processing speed or, in extreme cases, shuts down. Think, then, about what too much negative media with its emotional baggage is doing to you.

The same applies to the energy and esteem vampires in your life. You know—those who are constantly berating you with judgment and criticism, making you feel terrible about yourself. Decreasing your exposure to toxic people is just as important as decreasing your exposure to negative media.

Instead, perhaps it's time to focus four hours or so a day on consuming purposefully chosen educational and empowering books and programs, or meeting up with friends who also boost your view of life, or working through and tackling new challenges that remind you how strong and in charge you really are.

In terms of our personal happiness, the most important way to safeguard our outlook is to control our interpretations about how positive and personal we view the events of our lives. This is the basis for discussing optimism and identity in most of psychology.

We'll start with optimism and why it's important to start controlling your thoughts so you become or remain an optimist. If psychologists have proven anything conclusively, it's that it's best to interpret the information and events of your life with an optimistic mind-set, viewing what you see, hear, and experience as more positive than negative.

Being an optimist means that you view things in a good light and remain hopeful and confident that things will turn out well for you. When bad things happen to you, optimism helps you keep things in perspective. That's why optimists tend to view negative events in their lives as temporary, specific to one situation, and something they didn't necessarily cause but can handle or resolve.

Despite popular misconceptions, optimists aren't just dreamers who don't see the world as it is. In fact, optimists are *more likely to see the world as it is* and take action to address problems than pessimists are. That's because pessimists don't believe that problems can be resolved, whereas optimists do and, thus, are more willing to take action. Optimists in general have been found to be happier, live longer, cope better, last longer in loving marriages, and live healthier lifestyles. Pessimists tend to see negative events and experiences as things that will last longer, that will wreak havoc on their lives, and that cannot be controlled or stopped.

To those who say, "Well, I wasn't born an optimist," or, "I'm not wired that way," there's hope; neuroscientists have proven over and over again that new neural pathways can be formed (and old ones strengthened) by the conscious focus of our attention and deliberate practice. Without question, all normal functioning human beings can become eternal optimists with focus and effort. It's ultimately a matter of choice. So given the choice, what say you—a life of positive outlook or negative expectation?

The other major interpretation we make, and should control to safeguard our outlook, is how we relate events and incoming information to our self-concept—our identity. Those in a caged life often view incoming negative information and life experiences as evidence that they are "bad" or "not worthy." Those in a comfortable life feel like they "are not enough" or should have personally prevented problems from arising in their lives. But those living a Charged Life tend to see information as just that—information. They don't attach negative emotion and judgment to themselves just because someone says something negative, or something negative happens in the world. They protect their self-image and realize that a sometimes chaotic and volatile world need not shake their own internal constitution or perspective on how magical the world can truly be.

This internal power to safeguard and direct your outlook is the same force that allows you to shape and determine your character.

One of the most defining choices you can make in your entire life is deciding to control the quality of person you will be on an everday basis. What will you stand for? What kind of positive values, standards, and beliefs will you demonstrate each day? How much honesty, integrity, fairness, and kindness will you insist upon when meeting the world? This is the stuff of character.

Beginning today, set an intention and a relentless focus on living your life as the greatest person you can be, in all situations. Demand that you demonstrate a strength of character in such a way that you find pride in who you are, and that others see you as a role model.

You cannot control everything in life. But you *can* control *you*—who you are being, how you are treating others, what purpose is driving you. Controlling the quality of your character in a day-by-day, interaction-by-interaction, situation-by-situation kind of way is what fashions and forms the quality of life you will live, and your legacy too. When my dad was coping and fighting with cancer, I remember my entire family being in awe of how he remained so strong, so true to himself, so demonstrative of how gracefully we can meet any challenge. His character and his resolve to be a good human being throughout his life and all the way until his death inspires me to this day.

My dad's example reminded me, too, that character is not just who we think we are and what we stand for—it's what we demonstrate to the world. Intentions are not enough; our actions define who we truly are. In this way, nothing changes in your life until you change your behavior, demanding and showing more of your magnificent character. So challenge yourself on a continual basis with this question: "Do my actions reflect the quality of person I want to be, and can be?"

I remember meeting a very happy ninety-year-old volunteer at a nonprofit event for youth. After seeing this woman work joyously for nearly two hours with a group of elementary-school kids, I approached her and struck up a conversation about life. Something about her exuded a level of character that was palpable. At one point I said, "How do you have so much energy, and how do you have such incredible influence with those kids?" Her reply, which I quickly scribbled on a napkin afterward, changed me forever. "Brendon," she said, "all the energy and influence we ever want in life is *controlled* by one thing: *whether or not we are purposefully acting as our highest selves*. From that place of character flows grace and love, and in that place we find happiness and meaning" (italics mine).

Activator #2: Control for New

I have a friend named Paulo Coelho, the international bestselling author of beloved books such as *The Alchemist*, *Eleven Minutes*, *The Valkyries*, and dozens more. If you were to look at his life from a distance, he seems to have it all.

People all over the world recognize him. A jetsetter, he bounces around to his homes in France, Switzerland, and Brazil. His work is engaging and deeply fulfilling, transforming the lives of over half a billion people. More than nine million fans follow his every word online. Presidents and leaders of countries have acknowledged his contributions and have asked him to visit them in their capitals. His health is strong, and he was married for more than thirty years to the woman, he knows in his soul, he was meant to be with. A deeply spiritual and accepting man, his own journeys of self-discovery and search for meaning in life were exactly what had made him rich, famous, and loved. But over time, slowly but with surprising depth, he became, quite simply, miserable.

How could this be? Was this just an ungrateful man? No. When I spoke to him on his sixty-fifth birthday, I could tell he felt more than blessed in life. He was truly honored to have what we all want: love, security, respect, abundance, and a career of creativity and meaning. What, then, could possibly be going on in his soul and brain that would leave him so unsatisfied? His story and struggle to find the answer reveal a lot about life and, coincidentally, neuroscience.

Paulo is allowing me to share his story here, and he also detailed his crisis of faith and satisfaction in his brilliant book *Aleph*. He and I approached the issue from different perspectives—his spiritual one and my high-performance angle—yet we arrived at the very same conclusion: Paulo needed more *new* in his life.

In *Aleph*, Paulo describes how he came to believe that his crisis in faith stemmed from his not venturing into the world anymore. Yes, he traveled the globe, but it was from one safe cocoon to another, where everything was planned out and there were few new challenges or opportunities. He wasn't having new adventures, meeting new people, or being stretched enough to feel engaged. The grooves of his routine had deepened into a spiritual rut.

Paulo wasn't sure exactly what he was looking for, so he followed the coincidences in his life and committed to doing something new. This led to a journey across the entire continent-wide span of Russia via the Trans-Siberian Railway, an arduous adventure that introduced him to a woman who helped him find that something he'd been looking for all along. I'll leave the rest of the story to his book, but what ultimately helped him get the charge in his life back was challenging himself to explore himself and the world in new ways. This simple act of what I call "control for new" was what ultimately reenergized his mind and soul. And I'm happy he reconnected with his faith and found the charge again—he is my favorite author of all time, and I look forward to everything he does.

"Control for new" is a phrase I use with clients that seems to stick. It means that we should spend as much time strategically planning the introduction of new things and experiences into our lives as we spend planning for what we'll eat, when we'll work out, and how we'll accomplish our goals. Much of the boredom, depression, misery, and emotional malaise in life can be remedied by this concept of "control for new," and recent advances in neuroscience prove why.

After peering into thousands of people's brains with advanced imaging machines such as the MRI, neuroscientists have concluded that the brain is hardwired to seek and enjoy novelty and challenge. Remember those two ingredients: *novelty* and *challenge*. You can have all the right fixings for an incredible life—love, respect, abundance, and so on—but without these two ingredients your recipe ends up as a bland soup of sadness and disengagement.

Your brain becomes much more activated when something novel or challenging occurs. Novel things make your mind snap to attention and become sharp, releasing dopamine and energizing your brain to go into "let's figure this out" mode. It's what motivates us to learn. If that novelty also challenges us, then our brains stay engaged for even longer. And an engaged brain is a happy brain.

Interestingly, neuroscientists aren't the only ones, or the first, to prove this. Famed psychologist Mihaly Csikszentmihalyi essentially concluded the same in his seminal work on "flow" experiences. He found that happiness was most often reported as a state in which we lost track of time and were completely absorbed in something we enjoyed and had skills for but that also had new-enough elements to challenge us.

Of all the things you seek to control in life, it turns out that one of the most important ones is the introduction of *new*. Not doing so has dramatic repercussions: a bored brain, a restless soul. And like Paulo, no matter how much you have in life, it won't be enough without this one thing.

Controlling for new doesn't mean you must incessantly cram new things into your life each day. Lord knows, very few of us need to add even one more new thing to our already-long laundry lists. As with most things in life, though, it's not about quantity but, rather, quality. You should endeavor to add satisfying new experiences into your life consistently. For some people, that means something as simple as going to a new restaurant once a week. For others, that could mean learning a new skill or simply meeting new people. Controlling for new doesn't mean radically overhauling everything about your life. But small changes can have enormous impact and might be the very thing you need on your path toward a Charged Life.

Bottom line: setting your sights on enjoying new experiences regularly is one of the greatest ways to remain fully engaged, energized, and enthusiastic throughout your lifetime. Here are a few ideas to jump-start your focus on *new*:

Six Simple Ways to Control for New

1. *The ninety-day getaway.* Every ninety days, plan a getaway either by yourself or with your spouse or significant other. Yes, *every* ninety days. This doesn't have to be a trip around the world—the goal isn't how far you travel; it's how far you

get away, the difference being measured not in the miles you travel but in how far mentally you can break the monotony of routine in order to relax and rejuvenate. Take a "staycation" at home or, better yet, leave your home for one to five days and go somewhere new and disconnected. Some people will balk at this, saying, "That's impossible." To which I reply, "Oh, I thought you to be a much more creative and resourceful person, especially in improving your life." If you really value getting away, you'll make it happen—it's just four times a year, anyway, and you ought to be doing that for yourself.

2. *The restaurant or dining tour.* Make your date nights an excursion to a new restaurant once a week. If you're in a small town, get a group of friends to host dinner every few weeks. The goal is to get about town and experience new dining experiences.

3. *Shows, sporting events, experiences.* What's happening in your city this weekend? Are there shows or performances you can go see? Any new exhibits or exhibitions? Despite the fact that many of us love going to the movies, sporting events, or the theater, most of us rarely do. Make it a habit to be on the lookout for things you can go see and cheer for.

4. *Travel adventures.* Do you have a list of the top-fifty destinations you want to go to in your life? Are you actively checking them off the list, at least one per year? If not, get to it. Traveling is one of the surest ways to introduce healthy novelty, engagement, and excitement into your life. Make a point of saving up money and vacation time so that you are able to make these adventures a reality. The main rule to observe when visiting new places: do something new. Don't

just stay in the resort or hotel—get out and about and aim for adventure.

5. *Expanding your peer circle.* It's funny how "making friends" is so important to us when we're young, but we lay off our efforts the older we get. But your friendship and peer circles are the most important external influences in determining your happiness (outside of your intimate relationship). Get serious about expanding your peer circle by going to networking events, fund-raisers, and local events and performances. Be on the lookout not just for networking purposes, but for friendship-making purposes.

6. *Skill development.* What ten new skills should you develop this year? How actively are you currently chasing and working toward mastery of something like writing, speaking, singing, cooking, programming, leading, playing soccer, or some other artistic, athletic, or professional skill? The challenge of seeking new skills is one of the surest ways to test and transcend your own boundaries. Go find something new to learn, and fall on your face trying to learn it. Enjoy the process of learning—it's one of the easiest paths to a more engaged brain (and life).

These are just a few ideas for you. Personally, I implement them all with a relentless focus in my life, because I care enough about my energy, engagement, and enthusiasm to do so. It's not always easy, but as you will undoubtedly discover, variety is indeed the spice of life.

Activator #3: Control Workflow

When asked about an area of life that people wish they could have more control and satisfaction in, work and career always top the list. This, despite decades of advances in management and career-development theory and practice. We know more now than ever before about what makes happy workers and happy workplaces. Just visit your local bookstore, and you'll see hundreds of titles on career, management, culture, leadership, good business, and workforce effectiveness. We've figured out how to create fun and funky workplaces, "flatten" and decentralize organizations, outsource non–mission-critical tasks, collaborate across functions, share best practices, work remotely, attend meetings virtually, and so on. And yet less than 20 percent of workers worldwide say they are actively engaged and enjoying their work.

If you've ever worked for a large organization, no matter how well it is led or how well it's doing in the marketplace, you can sense in your coworkers and yourself an unspoken restlessness for more control and meaning at work. What gives? How is it that, with all we know about working smart and well, so many of us aren't happier, more engaged, or more productive at work, whether as employees or entrepreneurs?

I've spent almost fifteen years of my life studying this question in my high-performance work, and I've come to believe that the answer lies in two relatively recent arrivals to the modern workforce: *lack of ownership* and *distraction*.

For the better part of mankind's history at work, life was about accomplishing singular tasks. From the beginning of time the world was full of farmers and artisans, and they controlled the basic inputs and outputs of work, from beginning to end. The farmer planted the seed and nurtured and harvested the crop. Artisans forged raw materials into products. You owned your work, and you did the same thing pretty much year in and year out, for your whole "career."

Hopscotch to the mid- to late-twentieth century and observe the one singular management philosophy that destroyed all that. It was an idea intended to make our organizational lives more productive, and there is no doubt that it worked. The only problem is, despite its success—and it still works today—no one noticed that it was the thief in the night that robbed us all of more enjoyment at work.

The culprit? The project-based, cross-functional team. Beginning in the 1950s, as conversations about "scientific management" truly built up steam around the globe, the organizational world swiftly moved from tasks to projects. No longer did you work in your own little silo in the organization, and no longer did you own a job from beginning to end. Instead, you worked in teams from across the organization on various projects. This model is still the dominant reality of our organizational lives today, and its repercussions for your happiness will shock you. It turns out that the project-based, cross-functional team life has robbed you of something you didn't even know you valued as much as you do: ownership.

When I was pitching this book to potential publishers, I knew they would understand its ramifications if I could relate it to their lives. To do so, I asked, "Have you ever worked on a book project where you were sort of in and out of multiple meetings on it, and then the book became successful, and you and the team were very happy about it?" To this, everyone said yes. Then I asked, "And have you ever worked on a book project that you really ushered from beginning to end and took as your baby, and then the book became successful, and you and the team were very happy about it?" To this, too, everyone replied yes. Then the kicker: "Which of the two felt better? Which had you more engaged and left you feeling more satisfied and fulfilled?"

Of course you know the answers I heard. Everyone, without exception, valued the experience in which they were personally involved, shepherding a project from beginning to end.

Consider how this example transcends and applies across all contexts. Being more involved in a project from beginning to end is more satisfying than just popping into it for part of the time. Being fully invested in seeing your baby project grow up and come to fruition is one of the greatest joys of work. So build it in.

Project-based, cross-functional teamwork is not going to go away. But without getting into fortune-telling, I can guarantee one thing: *your level of engagement and enthusiasm will skyrocket when you decide to participate only in projects you can be fully invested in and be a part of from beginning to end.*

Of course, some will argue that they have no choice at work, that their projects are simply piled on their plates and they must be just a part of them. These folks will say that what I am asking is unrealistic. But I promise that no matter what your work environment is like, this is possible.

I'm suggesting that you control this area of your life, even if it means making sure you are in on at least two to five major projects a year that you are fully invested in. You can do that—either find those projects, ask for them, or create them. You'll be thankful you did.

If the first part of controlling for workflow is to control *what work you do*—and now you know that means increasing the number or quality of projects that you can be truly involved in from beginning to end—then the next part is controlling *how* you work throughout the day. This is the "flow" part of workflow, and we've got to get this right for you, starting tomorrow morning. And this is where we talk about what's preventing you from being a high performer. It's time to talk about distraction.

If the thief of ownership in the work world is the project-based, cross-functional team, then the bad guy in terms of distraction is—yes, you guessed it—email and text/instant messaging. I've asked audiences from around the world what's the number one thing they *hate* about work, and the answer is often their email. This makes a lot of sense, and it's probably why I'm so often quoted for a quip I make onstage: "The in-box is nothing but a convenient organizing system for other people's agendas."

If email is one of your top distractions or dissatisfactions about work, then it's time to take charge of that area and better control it. Email is just one piece of a larger problem: you're not controlling your entire day well, and you're not performing at the level where you deserve to be (and, these days, *need to be*).

Instead of going into theory or background, let me simply lay out how you should tactically work through your day. This approach, which we've taught at High Performance Academy for years, is one of the most popular time-management strategies I've ever taught. I call it the 1-Page Productivity Sheet, and it illustrates an entirely new way to go through your workday. (You can download this resource at www.TheChargeBook.com/resources.)

Whenever you start your workday—and, ideally, before then you have walked or exercised, said your prayers or meditated, and eaten a healthy breakfast—I recommend you immediately go into *strategy mode*. Do not open your in-box when you first get to work; if you start with your in-box, you immediately relinquish control—and your day's agenda—to others.

In strategy mode, your job is to think big picture about what you are trying to achieve and the main *projects* you are working on. So the top row of the One-Page Productivity Planner gives you room to write out the big projects you're working on and encourages you to brainstorm the three-to-five biggest moves you would need to take to bring each project to fruition.

Once you've completed this top row of the sheet (and, yes, I insist that my clients actually fill out the sheet by hand at the beginning of every workday), then it's time to switch into operations mode in the next two rows on the planner. The middle row is to help you think of the *people* you need to reach out to today, because either (a) you're waiting on a decision or information from them or (b) you need to share a decision or information. The bottom row is for setting priorities about what you absolutely *will* accomplish today, no matter what.

As simple as filling out the planner sounds, its effectiveness stems from what you do next. You're going to work the day in a very specific way, and in doing so, you'll finally master your in-box—and your ability to get things done.

After you've filled out the planner, you'll begin your day in the middle section, the *people* section. This is the first time you'll be allowed to enter your in-box today, and it will require substantial willpower to do so only as instructed here. This is what I want you to do: Open your in-box. Look for emails from ONLY those you are waiting on for a decision or information (which is what you wrote down in the middle section of the planner). Read and respond to their emails only. Once you've done that, then send out any emails you need to send based on what you wrote down in the people section. That all should take no more than twenty to forty-five minutes max. Now the critical part: Close your in-box and quit your email application completely. You are not allowed to look at it again unless there is spare time at the end of the day, period.

So if you're not doing email for the rest of the day, what are you doing? You're producing, which is the very root of the word "productivity." You're knocking off all the priorities you wrote in the bottom section of the planner. That's the rest of your day, and you will not check email again until all those items are finished. (If any of those items require emailing, then do them during the last hour of your workday only). Your job the rest of the day is to create real things, get real things done, make a real difference—not email like an addict. So focus on finishing your priorities. If you finish them early, do *not* open your in-box yet. First ask, *Is there anything else I can do right now to move one of my big projects forward even faster and more effectively?* If your answer is yes, do that until the last hour of your day. Only during that last hour of the day are you again allowed to check or send email.

Your challenge at work: don't allow yourself to be weakened

and distracted by checking your in-box all day. Spend most of your day actually completing your projects and priorities, which should always be about getting done real things that matter. Take back your agenda and make magic happen during the day. This will make you feel like you are back in control of your worklife, and it will explode your productivity and enjoyment at work.

Of all the things we can control in our lives that move the needle in making us feel the most charged, here they are: controlling our outlook and character, controlling for new, and controlling work-flow. In these areas lies our ability to maintain a great attitude and live with integrity, experience the magic and variety of the world, and direct our own agendas in positive and productive uses of our time every day. And should you be disciplined in doing so, you shall awake each day to a more magnificent and fully Charged Life.

CHARGE POINTS

1. If I were to live at a higher level of character and maintain a more positive outlook, I would have to begin . . .

2. Two things I could schedule in my calendar right now to "control for new" and introduce novelty and challenge into my life are . . .

3. A project that I could get involved in or create immediately that would allow me to be more fully invested in my work and shepherd a project from beginning to end would be . . .

Chapter Three

THE DRIVE FOR
COMPETENCE

*A person who doubts himself is like a man who would enlist in
the ranks of his enemies and bear arms against himself.*
—ALEXANDRE DUMAS

I just feel stupid a lot, and incapable of getting things done or
achieving my dreams."

Sitting on a lounge chair next to me, flicking at her fingernails,
was one of the most successful women I had ever known. To most
people in the world, Susan's statement would have seemed surprising. Here she was, an Ivy League–educated woman with a list of letters and certifications behind her name that would impress anyone.
She hadn't just climbed the corporate ladder; she bounded up it with
an enthusiasm and boldness that inspired her peers and leaders. Her
female counterparts looked at her as a role model. She led teams of
people all over the world. Rich beyond description, she had vacation
homes in several countries. She was a beautiful woman with a supportive and sensitive husband whom everyone loved.

I asked Susan a few questions, and we got to the root of the problem quickly. In the past year and a half, she felt she had stumbled
at work, losing her motivation and giving up too quickly, too often.

She wasn't taking risks anymore. She also had what her psychiatrist called "performance anxiety," for which he prescribed a medication, but it didn't seem to help.

"I don't feel like I'm learning as fast as I used to, now that I've had some success," she said in a defeated tone. "But, worse, I don't feel like I'm good at learning anymore, so I'm not taking on any big challenges or projects. Failure now concerns me more than ever. I keep avoiding taking action on too many things, letting myself get distracted as an excuse not to try, so I won't fail. Do you think I've lost my edge?"

I notice how terribly uncomfortable Susan is sharing this with me. My immediate instinct is to answer and comfort her, to tell her she's just imagining things, that everything will be okay. But she's not paying me to console her.

"Maybe I've just maxed out my ability or intelligence or something, Brendon," she went on. "I used to feel so sure, but now I'm feeling helpless, almost out of nowhere. So what can I do to get my confidence back so I don't feel so incapable anymore? What happened to me? This feeling is scaring the hell out of me, and it will destroy my career."

I now have two options once again: console or coach. One involves making a person feel better. The other involves making a person *be* better.

I take the risk. I sit up, turn to face her, and say with an out-of-context directness, "Susan, this may be the most ridiculous conversation I've ever been in with someone at your level."

She blinks back surprise and opens her mouth but says nothing.

"You're telling me that you're *waiting* to feel like a good learner again before taking on any challenges? That's like waiting for the car to start without putting the key in the ignition. You've got this all backward. You haven't maxed out your ability or intelligence, because, frankly, you haven't even been testing it."

I know, most people would think this is a horrible approach I'm taking. But I know her. I smile broadly as I'm saying this, but I also watch to see if she'll lash out. She doesn't respond, so I keep at it.

"You're unsure of yourself precisely because you're not *being* yourself anymore. You're not *pushing* yourself to learn and try new things, and that's the problem. If you're waiting for someone to smack you with a smart stick and tell you you're competent enough to try learning and risking again, then listen to me now. I don't think you've lost your edge; I think you simply stepped away from it because you got a little intimidated and a little comfortable. You got scared of your success, and you stepped away from the boldness that made you learn and made you feel alive. But you've leaped the edge before, right?"

"Yes. But maybe I'm just too tired of leaping and learning all the time."

"Well," I say, "maybe I'm hearing you wrong, but it seems to me that right now all your complaints are precisely because *you don't feel* you're leaping and learning anymore. We have a choice right now. We can go dig into your past and figure out all the excuses you have for not wanting to live and learn anymore. *Or* I can whop you with my smart stick, give you some challenges to make you learn and grow, and whop you some more until I push you over the edge again and make you soar. What do you want to do right now?"

She thinks for a moment. "I want to get my mojo back."

"Will you bring that mojo back by doing nothing, or by putting your ass out on the line again so that you can stretch, learn, and grow—be the best of you?"

She smiles again, this time fully. Her eyes say it all: *bring it on.*

· · ·

If you knew her, Susan's comment about feeling "stupid" and "inca-pable" would have surprised you. She is an amazing human being.

But everyone—all of us, without exception—feels incapable in many areas of our lives, stuck at different stages in our lives, and in different situations in our lives. Susan gives me an in to discuss one of the most important human drives: *competence*.

I hear Susan's story all the time because of my profession, but also because it's part of the human story. At some point, we all feel what she felt, because we all have the drive for competence fueling us. When we feel competent and capable, the world is ours. We boldly set out into the unknown, we adapt and learn readily, we conquer our fears and meet our challenges, and we experience heightened levels of confidence, success, and mastery. In coaching, we often refer to it as the "competence-confidence loop"—the more competence you have, the more confidence you feel in trying new things and taking on new and bigger challenges; the more you do that, the more mastery you develop and the more competent you feel.

But the second our internal competence scale tips from self-assured to self-doubting is the moment we begin feeling defeat. We start questioning our ability, intelligence, strengths—our entire future. When we feel inadequate, uncomfortable feelings such as anxiety, anger, disappointment, hopelessness, and fear of failure become the norm. The net effect of feeling incompetent is disastrous: we stop trying, learning, growing, and contributing. We start compulsively comparing ourselves to others, and we feel we don't measure up. Our charge in life can feel lost altogether because progress feels daunting, if not impossible.

I know you recognize many of these feelings. We've all felt them. And I also know that if we sat down for a few moments and had a heart-to-heart about the level of charge you feel in your life right now, I'd quickly learn that there are too many areas of anxiety and apathy in your life—two great symptoms of a misfiring or misuse of your human drive for competence.

You'd think that in our modern world of abundance—where

education and information are both so prized and so available—our drive for competence is easily activated and developed. It's easy to learn and gain new capabilities in our society, right? After all, we have schools and education-focused government programs and nonprofit organizations galore. Liberal-arts schools encourage students to ask questions and "find their own paths." Corporations have human-resource departments focused on "human performance," "skill paths," and even "competence development." Creating a "learning organization" has been the catchphrase of management for more than a decade. The Internet has opened up the world of knowledge to all of us, for free. We all should feel smart enough, good enough, and capable enough. All would seem well and right when it comes to our competence in this world . . . wouldn't it?

But that's not the case. Our nation's student test scores continue their decline, and around half of the students who begin college never finish. At work most people feel that anxiety has become the "new normal" despite the human-resource department's mission to give employees the skills and competence they need to succeed. Entire companies and global institutions have been wiped out in recent years for what can be described only as a lack of competence (and perhaps ethics) on the part of their managements.

So what gives? To understand this, let's define "competence" more specifically, then look at how our society often deprives us from having more of it.

Personal competence can be loosely described as our ability to understand, successfully perform in, and master our world. *Understand. Perform. Master.* If I have confidence that I can do those three things when facing life's challenges and opportunities, then I tend to feel competent. I feel as though I can sufficiently use my know-how and skills to manage and succeed at the tasks in front of me.

Consider your career for a moment. Do you understand your role and goals at work, and do you have a firm grasp on the social structure there? Do you feel that you are fully knowledgeable about what it takes to win and advance? Do you feel you have the talent, knowledge, skills, and abilities needed to achieve your and your company's goals? And do you feel you are mastering your job, learning quickly enough, and contributing consistently at a high level of excellence? Your answers to these four questions say a lot about how competent you feel at work.

The challenge for all of us, at work and in every other area of our lives, is the modern pace of change. When so many people are seeing their roles change continually—*here's another restructuring and round of layoffs that will load more work on my shoulders*—it's hard for them to understand where they fit in. We have to learn more and learn faster than ever just to stay afloat. Just staying "in the know" at work is harder than ever amid the constant stream of change.

The team- and project-based work dynamic causes many of us to act in ways that actually impair our ability to learn, which is critical to developing competence. We want to impress our teammates—especially now that we all are so socially connected—so we do everything we can to seem as though we "have it together." That means we often don't ask for help when we need it. We hide our inadequacies and vulnerabilities for fear of being found out. We quickly multitask to please everyone, which doesn't allow for the depth of focus that leads to mastery. Worse, we avoid conflict so that our teams love us and we can keep up the image of the fun, collegial, and happy culture we're supposed to be creating.

It gets deeper. As "global teaming" and outsourcing become more and more the norm, we all have become accustomed to passing off any tasks that don't show our strengths to someone else, delegating away our very ability to try new things, develop weak areas, *learn*.

No matter your occupation, we're an on-the-go, socially connected workforce that is expected to be more productive, more creative, and, yes, happier than ever before. It's the setup for a great tragicomedy: change comes at breakneck speed, yet you're never supposed to feel unsure or distracted.

But this is no laughing matter. A lack of competence at work—or in any area of your life—can seriously hurt your future. Here's what educational psychologists and human-performance coaches know about competence.

1. *Your competence level determines what you will give attention to.* When you don't feel competent, you tend not to pay attention to problems, conflicts, or bigger challenges and opportunities—because you don't feel you can handle them. In this way, a lack of competence leads to more delay and procrastination.

2. *Your competence level determines your choice of tasks and activities.* When you feel capable and confident that you can understand, perform in, and master your world, you are willing to take on harder tasks. This, of course, generally leads to more learning and more success at work. If you feel incapable, you focus on the easier tasks and quickly become a slave to safety.

3. *Your competence level determines your effort level.* Hard workers believe they can create positive outcomes with their effort, so they try harder. It seems all too simple, but expert performance studies have shown over and over that if you believe you are competent, you will work harder (and, yes, smarter).

4. *Your competence level determines how adaptable and resilient you will be.* This one has surprising implications for how successful you will be in life and at work. Those who

trust their abilities to understand, perform, and master their worlds are more willing to adjust their courses if something isn't working. They get up faster when knocked down, because they take the knockdown as a lesson rather than a defeat.

5. *Your competence level determines whether you will lead or follow.* Can you imagine a more needed skill today than leadership? But who are the ones who take the reins at work and in life? It's those who believe in themselves and their abilities. They feel competent to handle challenges, even if it's a stretch, because they trust they will figure out the challenge with others as they pursue a new, grander vision. (Sadly, those who don't trust in their abilities to understand, perform, and master their worlds can rarely even see a grand vision for themselves or others, let alone actively, courageously, and consistently chase it.)

Our rapidly changing world requires that we push ourselves to keep up and continue learning and adding value. Thus, the learners—the people always looking to expand their experiences in order to learn more about the world and grow in their own skills—will inherit the new world. With so much on the line, how can we activate our drive for competence in a healthy and energizing way? What moves the needle the most in developing competence? Here are the three most powerful activators.

Activator #1: Assess and Direct Your Desire to Learn

The desire to learn and master our lives is critical to our confidence and happiness. If we approach learning with joy and enthusiasm, we tend to feel more confident and capable in life. And neuroscientists are now proving that the more we learn, the more our neural pathways strengthen, which leads to our ability to better anticipate and perform, which in turn leads to the pleasurable releases of dopamine in the brain.

Naturally, we all want to feel the kind of confidence and neural pleasure that comes from developing competence, but why then, don't more people take on more opportunities to learn in life? Why is it that people often fail to challenge themselves to learn new things and build newer and deeper competencies?

It's not because they're lazy. (That seems to be many commentators' answer these days.) No, people aren't developing more competency and becoming learning ninjas simply because they are unaware of how they're evaluating new learning opportunities. They say no to learning a new language, for example, without really knowing why they don't want to try. (The general answer, "It's too hard" or, "I don't have the time," is only part of the story.)

Here's what I've learned: if we're going to amplify your ability to gain more competence in any area, we have to assess *why* you want to learn and *what* would prevent you from not doing so. We also have to help you *choose* learning challenges that actually light you up and shape your future.

With that in mind, you should know that there are proven key indicators that reveal whether or not you will succeed in (or even try) any learning challenge. If you are aware of these indicators, then you can better shape your approach to learning, and thus growth, in life.

(At High Performance Academy, these areas are part of our Action Indicator Assessment, which you can download for free at www.TheChargeBook.com/resources.)

Future Identity

In determining if you will even try to take on a new experience or learning challenge, which is how you would develop competency, the key question you will ask yourself is, *Is this goal or activity relevant to my future identity?*

For example, if you're preparing for a test in college physics but you don't see yourself using physics in your future life, then you will be less likely to study hard in advance, seek to be present during the exam, or reflect on whether you can do better in the future. Knowing this, think about how hard you're working right now to learn new things. Not trying very hard? Well, it's likely because you don't see a compelling new future identity for yourself that would require new skill sets. What new knowledge, skill, or ability could you start mastering to become a higher performer at what you do and increase your success in life?

Intrinsic Value

Most of us are taught to learn for "extrinsic values," or external rewards offered by the world like the acquisition of money, power, and accolades. In the worst metaphor of all time regarding motivation, people refer to this type of motivation as "the carrot and the stick," with the stick being a punishment if you don't act in the desired way, and the carrot being a reward if you act in the desired way. The problem with this metaphor is threefold. First, it assumes that we are all asses. Second, it assumes that we are all asses who will do the desired thing if beaten. Third, it assumes that extrinsic motivations actually drive us at all.

Finding intrinsic value—meaning finding a meaningful connection—in something makes it personally motivating, which is very different from how most of us have been taught to think of motivation.

Researchers continue to prove that we are more driven by intrinsic rewards than extrinsic rewards, such as following our passions, doing what we enjoy doing, feeling proud of a job well done, collaborating with a great peer group, and contributing to something we find personally meaningful.

With all this in mind, what would you *enjoy* learning in the next twelve months? What types of things could you challenge yourself to do in order to feel more excited and proud, regardless of the external reward?

Utilitarian Value

This indicator asks, *Will I get something useful from pursuing this goal?* Utilitarian value has always been the realm of economists who believe, for example, that we purchase items because we know we'll get use out of them, and that the price we would pay for such an item correlates directly to how much use we expect to get out of it. In our focus on high performance, this value is often felt when you *know* that taking on a new challenge will result in a direct benefit to what you are doing. For example, if learning to code a webpage would help you be more efficient at your work and get you a raise, then there is utilitarian value in learning to do so.

So, what would be *useful* for you to learn in the next twelve months?

Opportunity Cost

In taking on this new goal or task, what will you be missing out on? Participating in any endeavor costs time, energy, effort, resources, and willpower that could have gone into something else. We need to be aware of this reality, as most of us make unconcious decisions based on fear that we'll lose something altogether if we focus on something else. We say, "I can't learn *X* new thing because that would mean I couldn't take the kids to school in the morning." Of course, that doesn't make sense, as learning something doesn't have to come at the cost of taking the kids to school, but that's how we think. For the most part, we tend to hurt our ability to learn by obsessing on such false dilemmas. So ask yourself, *What new skill have I wanted to learn but fooled myself into not learning by focusing on some imagined opportunity cost that may not be true?*

Delay Time

This asks, *How long do I have to wait to get the benefits of trying and achieving this goal or activity?*

Let's imagine you're going to learn a new language—say, French. If you start getting tutored next week but you're not actually going to speak it in conversation until you go to France five years from now, does this affect your motivation to learn? Of course it does. Human beings are horrible when it comes to delayed gratification, and the longer we have to wait, the less our motivation to learn and try.

What have you been delaying learning now because you don't think you'll get an immediate payoff? How far along in the process would you be now if you had gone for it the first time you thought about it?

Personal Control/Agency

Personal "agency" is a term psychologists use to describe how confident you feel in your ability to control your actions and shape the outcomes in your life. If you doubt that you'll take the consistent actions needed to succeed at something, you're clearly less likely to ever begin. And if you are willing to act but you don't believe your actions will make real progress and achieve the outcome you're after, you're also less likely to begin. Looking back to the last year of your life, were there times you didn't chase your dreams because you didn't believe you'd work hard enough to achieve them, or, if you did work hard your efforts wouldn't bear fruit? That belief decimates your dreams. So, in thinking of any new challenge, it's important for you to feel sure that you are in control of your destiny. What examples can you recall to remind yourself that your hard work and efforts pay off?

Social Support and Connection

Will people support you and provide direction and cheerleading when you attempt something new, and will you be able to create meaningful relationships along the way?

We all want to feel safe and assisted when we try new things, and we also want to feel as though our risks are going to be recognized and rewarded socially. That's why it's so important to think through how you can be supported when you start a new learning journey or challenge. Want to learn to run a marathon? Get around other people trying to do the same thing.

Do you let your social network know about the goals and achievements that excite you? How can you leverage your social circle or a new group of people to help you stay motivated at doing something new?

Bandwidth Belief

This asks, *Will I have enough time and focus to do a good job learning and doing this new activity?*

Here we meet one of the greatest challenges to our competence development in our modern world: we all feel that our plates are already full, so we take on smaller, bite-size tasks. All the busyness has led many of us to take on more administrative or basic projects because we feel that such tasks won't make us overextend ourselves, when overextension—challenging ourselves beyond our current capabilities—is the very thing that leads to growth.

What unimportant activities are you spending too much time on, which could be better utilized to try meaningful new things?

Resource Availability

Will you have the resources you'll need to successfully accomplish this goal? One of the most convenient excuses we use in not beginning a new task or activity is that we won't have what we need to succeed. Consider the number of people who want to start their own businesses. The rationale you hear from them for not beginning is usually one or more of the following: no time/equipment/product/systems/computers/websites/staff/money, and so on. Of course, these are important considerations in choosing what to do or not do in life. The challenge, as with all the indicators mentioned above, is that we often make these evaluations *unconsciously*.

What resources would you need in order to take on a new goal or challenge that you feel passionate about?

Autonomy

This indicator often explains why a lot of people in the work world won't volunteer for new projects. It asks, *Will I be given the trust and decision-making authority I need to feel as though I'm in control and able to make things happen?* If you feel that you have to get permission at every decision point or that you are constantly being doubted or given the runaround, you simply won't be motivated to play the game in the first place. Equally important is the fact that you won't feel ownership over your work if you have to get approval every step of the way, and therefore you'll be less invested in the outcome.

Who can you get "permission" and support from to go try something new? How can you position yourself to have more decision-making authority and freedom when taking on your next challenge?

I share all these indicators and questions with you to help spur your thinking about how you've been approaching learning challenges. If I were you, I'd use these indicators as a sort of checklist the next time you're planning to do or learn something new. Ask yourself the types of questions above and think through them. Doing so will increase your likelihood to take on and be committed to challenges that require you to stretch, learn, and grow—to become more competent.

Activator #2: Set a Real Challenge, Plan for Success, and Get a Coach

Are you at the same level of skill and mastery in any important areas of your life that you were at three years ago? In other words, are there any meaningful areas of your life where you don't feel you've grown?

I believe that if you are committed to growth in your life, then you've got to truly *focus on growth*. And that happens only by purposefully choosing new challenges that develop your competencies in the areas of your life that you care about. So let's do that now.

It's time for you to choose a few real, observable, and time-bound challenges that will advance your life. First, let's define those terms. A *real* challenge is one that involves a stretch goal—it won't be easy to accomplish. If you're looking for easy, you may as well stop here and go back to the mundane life. An *observable* challenge means that we can have another person watch your performance *throughout* the challenge. That person needs to have a view into your performance from beginning to end, whether you have certain check-ins along the way, or the observer is literally by your side or on the sidelines the entire time. Finally, you need a *time-bound* challenge—one that has definite starting and ending points.

Before we get into the model, let me share a few examples of these types of challenges. If you're a basketball player, the challenge might be to score ten more points than you ever have (real) during a real game, in front of your coach (observable), in the fourth quarter alone (time-bound). Or let's say you're a sales executive. The challenge is to double the sales (real) you bring into the business by visiting, live, and selling to your top twenty clients, with your manager in tow (observable), over the next five weeks (time-bound).

Both examples meet our criteria. They also illustrate another point: in both cases, these would be self-defined challenges. The ballplayer came up with the goal. The salesperson came up with the task. This is critical to the success of developing new competencies. *You must now be the driver of your challenges, from this day forward. Yes, life will throw many challenges at you, but you should give yourself even more.* I know that sounds counterintuitive. Most people are running from challenges in their lives, not chasing them.

I highly recommend that you develop short-term challenges. I encourage my clients to choose sixty-day challenges, forcing themselves to try to learn new things and improve in an incredibly short time span. This keeps them engaged and excited to see short-term growth. Of course, it's important to plan for long-term skill development, but nothing is more exciting than a short-term challenge, so be sure to set those up along your path. Consider taking on a speed-learning project, with a challenge to learn something in sixty days or less. Maybe you can learn to play five of your favorite songs on the piano or other instrument. Or perhaps you decide to learn to cook a new vegetarian dish every night for sixty nights. Or teach yourself to use that new system or tool at work you've been avoiding. Whatever learning challenge you choose, *push yourself.* You'll be thankful you did.

So what will be the next real, observable, and time-bound challenge you will create out of thin air? What challenge can you design for yourself for no other reason than to learn, grow, and build more mastery and competence? Take a few minutes now to write down some new challenges for yourself at home, at work, and beyond.

Now that you have your challenges, let me give you a few pointers on how to successfully meet them.

First, be a planner. Every day, millions of people around the world walk into a conference room unprepared for the big meeting. Athletes get comfortable and forget to study their opponents before the big game. Parents stroll into their kid's room without first strategizing how they'll talk about the latest bad behavior at school. Without preparation, dramatic growth and mastery are impossible. Sure, you can sometimes succeed without planning or preparing; it happens every day. People luck out, or they rise to the occasion in the moment. But by winging it, they don't grow or attain mastery. That's because dramatic growth and mastery over time—real competence development—takes strategy, just as winning a chess match or a football game does.

If you're really going to enjoy the process of learning and developing a deeper sense of personal mastery, then you've got to become a planner. Pick your challenge area, then go read everything you can on the subject. Interview and model experts in that area. Rally all your peers around you and walk them through your thoughts and strategies.

Most important, try to get an unbiased coach to support you with good guidance and feedback along the way. A coach doesn't have to be a professional life or business coach like I am; it can just be a close friend or mentor who can help you think through your planning and performance in any given challenge. If this is an important challenge for you, don't fly blind and don't go at it alone. The fastest way to get better at something is to have a coach tell you where you can improve. A third party watching you is important to skill development because you can't improve what you can't see—when you're in the picture, you can't see the frame.

Activator #3: Integrate Successes into Your Identity

A sense of pride and progress is crucial to feeling competent. But one of the greatest dangers of a rapidly changing world is that we rarely get to feel or register all the things we've accomplished and mastered before we're back on the field of learning. Just when we've finally figured something out, *bang*, we have to learn something new again. If we don't take time to give ourselves credit for what we've learned, then we'll never feel as though we've progressed.

This is about taking the time to acknowledge the progress we make on a daily basis even as we're focused on meeting the challenges ahead. Throughout your lifetime, you've had tens of thousands of wins. Most of them you've barely noticed, and that's a shame. You never gave yourself much credit for learning to ride a bike without training wheels because once you did it, a new ambition swept in to master riding faster and farther. You might not have patted yourself on the back when you got your first job out of school because you were too busy focusing on how much you were going to have to learn about the new work environment. While all these examples are simple, they illustrate the fact that we're always onto the next thing before recognizing what we just accomplished. And if we don't recognize what we've accomplished in life—even the small things—then we never *feel* accomplished. We don't feel more competent, capable, and confident today than we did yesterday or the day before.

This is one of the huge challenges Susan—the woman from the story at the beginning of the chapter—was having. She was an amazingly successful woman, but she didn't *feel* that way anymore; her eyes were so focused on her lofty ambitions in life that she never recognized the remarkable results she was getting in the present moment. Nothing ever felt good enough, because she never even recognized the small steps she was making toward her grander dreams. Susan simply wasn't letting herself feel the wins.

One of the most influential exercises I gave Susan to recharge her life was to sit down and write out every accomplishment and achievement she had made in the past decade of her life. I had her write at least one page of "win memories" for every single year of the past ten years. The activity required her to consciously remember all the small successes she had had to get to where she was today. She had to write every new skill she developed that year, every book she could remember reading, every course she remembered taking, every performance appraisal she had that recognized her progress. The exercise was enormously challenging and time consuming, to say the least. She told me it took her nearly eight hours to complete, not because she had such a laundry list of wins to record, but rather because she had to rack her mind to remember them. When she sent me a scanned copy of all her pages of wins, here's what she wrote:

> Brendon, I'm writing you this email, crying my eyes out. This was one of the most powerful activities I've ever done. It was empowering in the end, but I have to tell you that it was miserable throughout. I say that because as I was going back over the last decade of my life, I had barely a scant recollection of everything I've achieved. I could so easily come up with what I'd guess you call "loss memories," but I really, really had trouble coming up with positive memories of feeling pride or achievement. That made me realize that I'd just never integrated my successes into my mind. No wonder I never felt like I was smart enough. I was just too blind to see I was getting ahead and getting better and smarter. Thank you for this. I hope you really enjoy reading my memories. It turns out these twenty pages feel like my first win in years.

I think you deserve the same gift. Take some time to do the same exercise for yourself. Trust me.

It's likely that you have a daily planner or run your life based on the calendar on your computer. For most people, closing their calendars is one of the last activities they do every day at work, since they often look at it last to know what will be on their agendas for tomorrow. From now on, before you close your planner, take a moment to look at all you accomplished today. Don't think about what you *didn't* accomplish. Just think about what you did achieve, even if it wasn't changing the entire world in one masterstroke. I encourage you to close your eyes, think about all you've done, and simply say to yourself, *I'm progressing. One small step at a time, I'm progressing.* Allow yourself to feel a sense of pride and gratitude for what you've done today.

Let's go further. I'd like you to start keeping a personal journal. Perhaps you already do, so this will be just one small additional thing to note. If you don't have a journal, you should. Much of our sense of competence comes in *reflection* about our lives, not just about the actions we take. That's why I'd like you to start writing in your journal at least once a week and noting what you've learned and how you've progressed. Since Susan was so career- and workweek-focused, I asked her to keep her journal with her and on every Friday afternoon, before she left work, to write an entry about what she had learned during the week about herself, other people around her, and the world in general. To say this activity reignited her life would be an understatement. Along with the "win memory" activity above, she finally started viewing herself as a learner again. And if we can help you see yourself as a successful learner, then we can start making you feel more competent and, in the end, alive and accomplished.

CHARGE POINTS

1. One area I would have to develop more skill and competence in if I am going to make my dream future come true is . . .

2. A sixty-day speed-learning challenge I'm going to give myself is . . .

3. One of the ways I'm going to start celebrating my wins and integrating my successes into my identity is to . . .

Chapter Four

THE DRIVE FOR
CONGRUENCE

Don't compromise yourself. You are all you've got.
—Janis Joplin

Twenty-five minutes is all I have with Michelle. I know my time is short, so I lean forward, look her in the eyes, and ask matter-of-factly, "Is it possible that there is a more unique, bold, exciting, and expressive person in there?"

She seems stunned by the question. She's been crying, and I think she wants me to cry with her. But I am not her girlfriend or her therapist; I'm her coach.

For the past thirty-five minutes, Michelle has detailed why she should be happy but is not. Most of her emotional malaise in life, she says, stems from her childhood and her inability to "get it together" and be who she thinks she can be in life. She has laid out a very good case for why she feels that everyone in her past and present has dealt her a bad hand. Life isn't all roses, she reminds me, and she's trying so desperately to feel accepted, to fit in. Then she begins to cry as she chronicles more reasons why her life feels inconsistent with who she thinks she is and can be.

Thirty-five minutes already gone. In twenty-five minutes, at the top of the hour, she will walk out of my office and I will not see her again. I have been paid to turn her life around. It's a ridiculous challenge, but she knew my work and results and hounded me for one hour of coaching. I don't believe in overnight transformation, but she insisted, and she is here. And now I have twenty-five minutes left.

I don't think she likes the coolness of my approach. But I don't let up. I lean forward, just a few inches from her face, and peer inside her eyes with a look that says I'm searching for her soul:

"Is it possible that there is a more unique, bold, exciting, and expressive person in there?"

She looks of two minds about the question. "I don't think of myself that way. Not everyone is like that all the time. Well, maybe a part of me is like that, but I don't act like that, really."

I tilt my head, still looking in. "Perhaps that's the problem."

·   ·   ·

This is hard to say to people without offending them, but it's a universal truth even for the most high-performing people on the planet, so here it is: your self-image could be a lot better, and you ought to be a lot more congruent in how you engage the world.

How we think of ourselves (our self-image) and how we behave in accordance with that image in the real world is the stuff of congruence. It's one of the most profoundly powerful drives we have as humans—to live in consistent alignment with who we think we are, how we want others to perceive us, and who we want to become. When we don't behave as the person we believe ourselves to be, we feel "off," "out of sorts," and, often, frustrated or angry. If we think we're lions, for example, but we act as mice, we secretly loathe ourselves.

Michelle's challenge, as I discovered and coached her through, is the same dual-sided challenge of congruence that most of us have:

1. She thinks too little of herself, and it causes her to act that way in the world. She's congruent with her limited belief about who she is and thus feels miserable.

2. She also knows she can be more, and when she's not acting as her best self, she feels miserable. She's not congruent with whom she knows she can be and thus feels miserable.

Like all human drives, then, congruence can be positive or negative. It's positive when we have a good self-image, high standards, and congruence with that image and standard in life. But it's negative when we think small of ourselves and our behaviors fall in line with that image.

Indeed, that's the ultimate challenge of our human drive for congruence: most of us *are* congruent with how *small* we think of ourselves—we question our value so we act timidly in life—but we are *not* congruent in our everyday actions with how *great* we know we can be—we know we're patient and loving people, but we lash out at others.

The only way I've found to work through this challenge is to help people create higher standards and expectations for themselves and to insist they bring those standards and expectations into how they interact with the world. The mantra is, "Think more of yourself, and demand that your actions be congruent with the best of who you are and who you can be."

There's a lot at stake here. I'd bet that many of the roughest times in your life were when your actions weren't congruent with your thoughts, or when other people failed to be congruent with you. Recalling that time you blew up at your loved one, even though you think of yourself as a caring and patient person, probably still makes you feel guilty. Or that time someone said you could trust him but then stabbed you in your back—I bet you still remember that one. So it's important for you to be congruent for yourself *and* for others.

Of course, it's hard to always be congruent. Naturally, different parts of us are engaged at different times. We might be a rock star at work but a janitor at home. We may be fun, exciting, and playful with our best friends but shy and reserved in bed. We can be aggressive in one situation, then fail to be assertive when it counts. Variation in who we are in any given context is natural and, despite what some would have you believe, healthy. Life would be terribly unhealthy (and boring) if we were exactly the same all the time.

Still, you can't create congruence with something you've never defined, so it's important to consciously create a unifying self-image of who you are and who you want to be. Setting standards for yourself is the best way to do that, so we'll begin there.

Activator #1: Set New Standards for Yourself

In today's world, our identities and standards are often crafted by external influences. We are constantly bombarded with messages about how to be cool, accepted, loved, and successful—how to behave so we fit the mold. What to wear, how to act, when to speak up, what's possible—all this information enters our imagination and, if unchecked, our identities and expectations for ourselves.

Who has crafted your self-image and standards in life? Has it been your family and friends? The media and society at large?

It's easy to dismiss these as leading questions and say, "I'm not defined by others." And to this, I agree completely. My simple question is, *Then who has defined you?* How much hard work have you done, consciously and deliberately, in deciding who to be? Most important, are you acting each day in congruence with your self-defined image, so that you feel authentic, proud, complete, fulfilled, and trustworthy to show up in every situation as the unique, gifted, true you?

Most people are living self-images and sets of standards that were developed by events and people from their pasts. Here's what I believe about the past: your self-image today shouldn't be all that tied to it. I don't believe that how other people have treated you in the past should be entangled in how you view others or choose to be as a human today. The past can be just a convenient dumping ground for unmet expectations. *(She should have treated me this way, not that way; I should have been better cared for; I wish I had done this or that.)* But we must always view the pains or disappointments from the past with mature, conscious, and self-determined minds in the present. When recalling anything from our childhood experiences, for example, we should be vigilant in reminding ourselves that all meaning, association, and integration that attached to it was made through the undeveloped psyche of an innocent and immature child. As children, we think *we* are the cause of the actions for and against us, even when that's not the case. A child is not responsible for a parent's hitting or cursing at or otherwise abusing him or her—that is on the parent. But a child doesn't have the objective viewpoint of a mature observer who could easily say, "Your parents are unsafe and untrustworthy." And even if a child were told this, in his or her developmental stage he or she could not process the concept "my parents are 'bad.'"

But this isn't just about childhood. Any influence from any time in our pasts may be a convenient explanation for why we think and behave as we do today, but there is a vast difference between an *explanation* and an *excuse*. At some point in our conscious adult lives we have to face the uncomfortable reality that *our self-image is and always has been chosen by no one other than ourselves.* That's why I say it's time we removed all past doubts and limitations on who we can become—we just don't have any excuse. It's as Erica Jong said: "Take your life in your own hands and what happens? A terrible thing: no one is to blame."

Our view of the past is further colored by the lens we use to look back on it. When pondering how the past affected us, we don't look for *our* effect on *it*. We think about what we were up against versus what we stood for. We remember what we feared but not what we dreamed. We ponder how much we were loved versus how much we loved. We think, *Why did all that happen to me? What did I get out of it? Where will it lead me?* when perhaps we should wonder, *What did I make happen? What did I give? Where will I direct myself now?*

I bring all this up because in the end our self-image is a self-fulfilling prophecy—remember, our human drive makes us behave in accordance with that image. So if you're running your life based on an old, outdated, past self-image shaped by others' opinions and actions, then you're in big trouble.

If that's true, then your efforts *starting today* should go toward defining *who you are today and who you want to become*, not by living from your past but, rather, *living into y*our future.

Let's use that focus to our advantage and set our intentions on who we want to be in life. Then our behaviors are much more likely to follow our own standards.

I often ask my clients to choose and memorize six words that become the standard frames through which they act in life: *three words about who they are* and *three words about how they treat others*. Since we live in a social world, those seem to be two good categories of standards to set—who we are and who we are with others. While choosing just six words to help us stay congruent might seem a simple activity—especially after all we've covered in this chapter—it's actually one of the most important things you'll do in your lifetime. Without having a set intention and standard for how to behave, we are driven by nothing but our immediate animal impulses to fight, flight, or freeze. By purposefully choosing our character and behavior, though, we soar to our highest potential as conscious beings.

Let's begin by selecting and committing to three words that will, from now on, define the trait of who you are as a person. A trait is generally thought of as a consistent characteristic in your nature, and by defining the words of who you want to be, you will be more likely to enact that trait in life. That's congruence at work.

Please take a few minutes now to brainstorm a bunch of words you might use to *define yourself* in your personal life from now on, and jot them all down below. Note: these are words that are just for you and how you think of yourself. These don't have to be words about how you interact with other people—that comes next. For now, just think about three words you want to define yourself so that you can use them to stay anchored in who you are.

- The words I would love to define the way I think of myself in my personal life are . . .

- Of all these words, the THREE that I'm going to make my standard and my mantra in how I think of myself are . . .

- I chose each of these three words because . . .

Don't continue reading until you've done this exercise (and no cheating!).

Once you have these three words, you might write them down on a notecard and carry them with you at all times. I've had clients post these on their computers, set daily calendar reminders to flash the words up several times a day, and even get them tattooed on their bodies. (I sure hope they were certain about those three!)

My own words for the past fifteen years have been *Present, Enthusiastic*, and *Bold*. I chose these words because I saw them as critical in helping me engage with life in the raw and real moments, seek new ideas and experiences in the future that made me look forward to each day, and challenge myself to be visionary and courageous. I remind myself of these three words multiple times a day—I've done it so many times consciously that it's now automatic that I think of these words, probably dozens of times per day.

Now let's move on to defining your *three social standards*. These are the words that you will keep at the top of your mind whenever you are interacting with another person. I say my three words to myself whenever I shake the hands of a stranger, call a client, lead my team, or greet my wife when she walks in the door. They're my all-encompassing reminder about how to behave in a relationship-driven world.

Please take a few minutes now to brainstorm once again.

- The words I would love to define the way I interact with others are . . .

- Of all these words, the THREE that I'm going to make my standard and my mantra in interacting with others are . . .

- I chose each of these three words because . . .

People often find this one easier than the first set of words because we all have so many social norms and expectations we grew up with. Make sure you thought through these and are using words that *you*, not someone else, chose. Be crystal clear on why these are the words specifically for you.

If I ever meet you on the street or at one of my events, these are the three words running through my head: *Engaged, Caring, Inspiring*. I chose these three words because I saw them as critical in helping me remember to demonstrate to other people that I am interested in them and in listening to them without distraction; that I deeply care about who they are as human beings; and that my greatest role with them is to remind them of what's possible and positive in their lives.

These six words, when internalized and demonstrated in the world, can have an immediate and long-term effect on your life. When I worked with Michelle, the woman from the opening story of this chapter, I had challenged her to be more unique, bold, exciting, and expressive. I did that because that was the opposite of how she was coming across to me. But I didn't want to dictate who she needed to be—too many others had done that for her. So I asked her to come up with her own words to describe her ideal self, the words that would from now direct her behavior. She had a tough time coming up with her own words. But when she did, I saw a miraculous physical change take place. She chose her personal words to be *strong*, *alert*, and *purposeful*. When I asked her to stand and walk around the room living out those words, she walked taller and more confidently.

Her social words were *honest, animated,* and *graceful.* This showed up immediately when I asked her to tell me a story about what her life would be like if she lived those words. Suddenly, this previously quiet and frustrated woman became very articulate and ambitious about what she wanted from life. She moved more, smiled more, seemed herself. She was no longer hiding out or acting like someone told her to act. Her whole demeanor changed simply because she was focused on new standards of being.

The ultimate power of this activator, as with all the others, comes from activating it consistently. If you write down your six words here but never remind yourself of them and fail to direct your behavior based on them, then it's all for nothing. It's one thing to see yourself as a person to whom all those words apply, but it's another thing to consciously set out to be that person with every action and interaction. Have a vision for who you can be and actually *be that vision*—that's congruence. When these words become your mantra and personal standard of conduct day in and day out, then you're more likely to be congruent with exactly the person you've always wanted to be. Psychologists have found that the more we can regulate our internal world to resonate with others, the healthier and more fully functioning we are. This strategy helps you do that by giving you a frame with which both to *view* and to *measure* yourself, your interactions with others, and, ultimately, your congruence in life.

Live your six words. Every day.

Activator #2: Set Your Mood Meter

Here's something most people don't think about: We sense congruence in our lives not only in how we *behave,* but also in how we consistently *feel.* If our emotions are all over the place, then we don't feel there is a congruence in our internal world. Constant emotional ups and downs beyond our control, driven by others or circumstance, make us feel miserable. Similarly, when we feel one way but always act another—say, we're sad but always forcing a smile—then our internal/external congruence feels off. Without a steady state of emotional reality, both felt internally and demonstrated externally in the social world, we feel out of harmony, incongruent.

On the flip side, if we have a positive, sustained, and *even emotional energy* about us, then we feel our emotions are congruent with how we want to feel in life. We feel grounded and secure in our emotional world no matter what the world throws at us. In this way, *feeling* congruent is sensed by having a consistent internal emotional set point or mood.

Our mood is our prevailing emotional tone, quality, or attitude. It's our steady, emotional energy about life. You can quickly gauge this overall tone by averaging how you tend to feel in life and how those closest to you would describe your mood. (Bringing in other people's opinions will keep you honest—for instance, by your saying, "Oh, I'm always happy," when your wife would call you a grump.)

Our emotional tone and energy aren't dictated by life's circumstances, and they aren't something we are blessed or saddled with at birth. As I am fond of saying, "The power plant doesn't *have* energy; it *generates* energy." We choose the color of our own sky.

Of course, we'd all like to live life in a positive mood. When we have that enduring emotional quality, we are more likely to be happy, inspired, relaxed, and able to enjoy life. Psychologists even find that those with a positive mood are more creative, resourceful, and resolute when facing life's challenges. But, oh boy, when we're in a negative mood, watch out. We feel more tense and intolerant, crotchety and critical. Our entire sense of ourselves and our world is cast under a darkened veil.

So what mood would you like to experience consistently?

How would you describe it? Why is that the mood you specifically want to experience? What could you do to stay conscious of your mood?

In staying congruent with the moods you want to experience in life, it's helpful to know what influences mood in general. Since moods are our overall enduring emotional tones, anything that affects our emotions can affect our moods. I've found that the most important factors to mood are physical movement (that's why, when you were in a funk, your mom used to say, "Why don't you go for a walk?"), sound or music (we all have songs that lift our moods), mental focus (pay attention to the negative, and that's how you feel), social vibe (we tend to meet the moods of others around us), and future orientation (if you feel enthusiastic about the future, you tend to feel that way in the present).

I've been using these factors *very* strategically as I cope with the concussion I've been dealing with since my ATV accident. I walk or exercise every single day. I have my favorite music playing through-out the house. I'm avoiding all negative media. I'm hanging out with fun friends and my cheery wife, and I'm keeping my eye toward a healthier and more thrilling tomorrow. These are all simple strate-gies for living in congruence with how I want to feel.

Here are more ideas you can implement on a daily basis to man-age and maintain a positive mood:

- Begin every day by asking yourself, *What am I looking forward to the most today, or what could I decide to do today that I can look forward to?* Starting the day with a positive expectation is key to setting your mood meter high.
- Drink a lot of water all day long—around six liters of water total if you are living an active and fit lifestyle. It turns out that most fatigue, hunger, and headaches—

all serious mood killers—stem from a lack of proper hydration.

- Look for reasons to say "thank you," and show appreciation throughout the day. Complimenting others and showing gratitude has been shown to elevate mood significantly.
- Have lunch with friends. Being around people you like and socializing with others always improves mood.
- Write in a journal each night, detailing the things you are grateful for from the day's experiences, as well as what you've learned and look forward to.

Finally, for the next thirty days, write an entry in your journal about your overall mood for that day and why you felt that way. Then brainstorm some ways you could have generated a more charged mood for that day. The act of writing this down every day will keep your focus and imagination on how you can finally start feeling the way you've always wanted to feel in life.

Activator #3: Keep Your Word and Follow Through

"Keep your word" is one of my favorite self-help mantras of all time. It just screams, "Be a good human!"

The mantra couldn't be any more straightforward and universally accepted as a good idea, yet few people do it. After all, how many people in your life fail to do what they said they would do?

What gives? Why, for example, do we commit in January to losing weight and then not do it? Why do we preach acceptance and then snicker about others at the water cooler?

The answers have a lot to do with our casual attitude toward the statements we make in life, which in turn stems from the consequences we attach to those statements. If we operate from a place that says, *My word in this world isn't important or inspiring to other people*, then we tend to be frivolous with what we say. But what if we imagined that our word is as significant a contributor to our legacy as our actions? What if we imagined that what we say is broadcast out into the collective consciousness of mankind? What if we simply pretended that our words and promises would be on the front page of the newspaper tomorrow?

Living from the intention that your word in the world is meaningful and that other humans rely on it for their sense of fairness, stability, and inspiration is the starting point to a better quality of life and a deeper sense of congruence. People really do relate to the world based on the words of others, which I'm sure you recognize after having done the exercises in this chapter. Words count. Words can inflict pain or inspire greatness. What becomes powerful is realizing that over time our words come to reflect who we are, and they either hurt or help the world. This is the place that I ask my clients to live from.

We have to go further. In addition to doing what we say in the world and understanding the depth of our own voices and their impact, we have to become hypervigilant about following through with our responsibilities. This is different from just "follow through with what you promise." Yes, we have to do that, but to feel completely congruent in our lives, we have to follow through on things we never even verbally promised. This is a critical distinction to feeling congruent in life.

Congruence isn't just in doing what we say we'll do but in doing what *we know* we should from start to finish. If you start painting your house and don't finish, there's something deep inside you that feels off until the project is done. Maybe that feeling doesn't live at the top of your mind as you go through every day of your life, but it certainly comes up whenever you think about your satisfaction with your home; it is unfinished spiritual baggage.

What are your responsibilities in life? What have you started but not finished? What can you do *today* to better manage your responsibilities and finish what you've begun?

This concept isn't just an isolated self-help principle. We've crossed a tipping point in our globally connected community when we've become hyperaware of meeting our promises and completing our responsibilities to one another. You can be part of the solution in this malaise of meandering commitments. You can inspire others with how solid and helpful and dedicated you are. You can, in the simple everyday actions of being a good human, inspire yourself.

As you can see, congruence is a big concept in your life. When your actions are congruent with who you want to be in life, how you want to feel, and what you think you should be doing and achieving, then you start to have a stronger internal constitition. You feel more grounded, responsible, sure. A new level of harmony and steadiness enters your life, and you feel proud of who you are and how you interact with the world. You barely blink at an unsteady and uncertain world, because you find steadiness and certainty within. *Life* becomes yours.

CHARGE POINTS

1. To live my six-word standards each day, the behaviors I would have to stop or start in my life to be more congruent with them are . . .

2. Three things I could do every day to better manage my mood so I can have a greater day-to-day congruence in how I feel are . . .

3. Five commitments I'm going to make and keep in the next sixty days are . . .

Chapter Five

THE DRIVE FOR
CARING

I expect to pass through life but once.
If, therefore, there be any kindness I can show,
or any good thing I can do for any fellow being, let me do it now,
and not defer or neglect it, as I shall not pass this way again.

—WILLIAM PENN

I don't think anyone gives a shit, and frankly I don't either. Next
question."

The man in front of me is a hulking dude. At six foot five, with
a barrel chest stretching the limits of his T-shirt, and biceps the size
of grapefruit, he looks as if he could toss me across the room like an
empty soda can. And by the red look of anger on his face, I worry
that he just might.

But I won't let him detach.

So I ask again, "So who cares about you, and who do you care
about?"

His eyes bulge, he tilts his head, and he looks at me with disbelief. "I'm not some touchy-feely metro from the city. I'm not here to
meet with you about 'caring'; I'm here to get to performing at the
next level. So next question, Coach, or I'm gone."

He's right; he's here to learn to improve his performance. A well-known former football player, he now sells cars. It's not a sad downgrade—his lots are making millions. He's one of the best but wants to be *the* best. Someone told him that I'm the guy who can energize people's lives. All he wants from our meeting are a few strategies to motivate his team and some "ninja mind tricks" to motivate people to buy more cars from him.

I've already sized the guy up. Most of his buyers are women. He's too aggressive. He doesn't come across as someone who cares. His brains, assertiveness, and name helped him climb the ladder, but he'll need to learn the truth we all stumble onto at some point: only the more humanly connected, caring, and emotionally engaged among us ever become number one at any endeavor (or truly happy, for that matter).

I believe that deeply. But in this moment I decide to detach emotionally. I decide to meet him on the battlefield. I risk it.

"Okay," I say, leaning back in my chair and eyeing him from head to foot, slowly so he can sense that I am measuring him up. "It takes a tremendous amount of guts and strength to talk about what you pass off as touchy-feely. Matters of the heart are matters of life. Maybe you've just got a hole in your heart or a block in your brain, but if you need a few minutes to psych yourself up like in a locker room or something, I'll be happy to sit here while you walk outside and muster up the courage to come back in here and talk to me like a real man with a *real heart.*"

People do not tend to speak that way to hulks like this, and when they do, it always knocks the hulk off balance. It also sometimes leads to a left hook.

There's only a split second of surprise in his eyes. Then he coolly leans forward. With a cold, neutral voice, the kind that only men who have fought in battle can use, he says, "Is that right?"

There is no noise in the room. No movement. Just a silence, a thickness of tension before the thunderclap. Just two men staring each other down, eyes devoid of humanity. Ready.

I don't blink. I don't know what will happen. My Hail Mary strategy is to let him know I "don't give a shit," so that, hopefully, he will start to.

Suddenly, he releases. He snorts, leans back in his chair, glances out the window, then back at me. His left lip rises in a coy smile even as he rubs his hands on his pants. "I guess we're gonna have to go deep, huh, Doc?"

This makes me smile. I'm not a doctor, and he knows it.

I let out my breath, too. My voice softens, and I look at him compassionately now. "I bet not many folks know how much you feel. You *care* about people a lot, don't you?"

He takes a deep breath and looks up to the right, thinking. Then, to my surprise, the giant tears up. "I *want* to," he says.

• • •

The capacity to care and be cared for is a human strength. It's what allows us to be nurtured as children, and it's what allows us to demonstrate love, empathy, kindness, forgiveness, and altruism with others as we mature.

In much of the academic and professional world, the word "caring" is often relegated to the nursing profession. Caregivers—those who give primary care to the sick, dying, aging, or incapacitated—are generally nurses or people who take care of their loved ones during hospice.

But I think of caring in a much broader way. We all should strategically focus on being better caregivers to everyone we meet in life. We should also be better care *receivers* by more readily attuning to and appreciating the caring thoughts and gestures from others. When we do, life lights up. (So, too, as you will see, do our brains.)

Almost everything you so desperately desire from others can

be sensed only by their demonstration of caring. You want attention, validation, acceptance, sympathy, respect, adoration, affection? Those show up in your life only if a person cares for you and demonstrates that caring in one of these ways. When others demonstrate their caring for you—by telling you they love you, touching you on the shoulder in tough times, sharing the warmth of a kind word—you feel recognized and appreciated by them.

When you don't feel cared for in life, trouble begins to brew at deep psychic levels. Babies who are not cared for die. Suicide notes ring with the haunting assumptions that "no one cared" and "no one will care." People without a caring environment demonstrate erratic behavior, lack positive emotional range, get divorced, cheat, and abruptly quit jobs. (The number one reason people quit their jobs, across all industries? Lack of appreciation—no one demonstrated that they cared about or were grateful for the person's hard work and contributions.) Caring is serious business.

There's a flip side, too. Beyond just receiving caring from others, when you don't demonstrate care to others consistently, life loses its color and connection. You feel less emotionally engaged with those around you. The hormones that regulate the development of social attachment—vasopressin and oxytocin, for instance—don't flood your head enough, leaving you feeling alone.

If you're not making a point to be caring of others in your life, the people around you don't feel cared for, loved, appreciated, respected, or engaged by you at the level of the heart. So, naturally, they contact you less frequently, trust you less, buy from you less, follow you less, and leave you more. In all human relationships, it's a remarkably easy formula to figure out: care more, connect more.

And yet caring is a separate human drive from connection (the subject of the next chapter). Our drive for caring is a need for a broad sense that we are safe, worthy, and loved, that by our own actions and the actions of others, we are cared for. Connection is more specific, about a sense of belonging and a type of relationship with others. A connection is something you have; caring is something you do and receive.

I'm betting that, if you're like most people, "caring" probably isn't something you've had on your radar for a while. If we looked at your daily planner over the past twelve months, I imagine we wouldn't find dozens of notations along the lines of "Demonstrate more caring today. Allow myself to be cared for, too."

So what gives?

In my view, of all our human drives, caring gets the least attention. People rarely talk about it at all. As such a profoundly powerful human virtue, you'd think it would be the focus of psychological conferences and bestsellers. Instead, caring's sexier sister, *Love*, gets all the fanfare, this despite the fact that it is probably impossible to feel or demonstrate love without caring. Even *Kindness*, caring's altruistic brother, gets more ink, this despite the fact that if you didn't care, you probably wouldn't bother to show kindness to another.

Because caring gets so little attention, it's easy to make giant leaps of progress in this area of our lives. Before I share a few activators to fire up your ability to give and receive care, let's explore *why* so many people feel cut off from the emotions of caring.

We're all hardwired to demonstrate care for others—but some of us have been cut off from our emotions and mental functioning in a way that blocks, or prevents us from giving, care. This, as you'll see, was the hulk's problem in the story above.

When I say "hardwired" to care, I mean that quite literally. It turns out that your brain is remarkably well equipped, biologically built to relate to and care for others' emotions and experiences. Essentially, your brain is built to mimic that which you see and feel in others. You've sensed this before when you walked up to a group of people and found them in a sad state. Your emotional range probably soon met theirs—a phenomenon that scientists call "emotional contagion." This happens because of a system of mirror neurons, which actively fire in a way that makes us sense and mimic others. They are called "mirror" neurons because they cause a logical and emotional response within us that mirrors what we see in others. All this happens automatically and subconsciously. Of course, we can choose to act or not to act on these neural firings, but remember the basics of brain science: the more the neural firings take place, the more the pathways are strengthened, and the more likely the same response in the future. So if we constantly see others behaving a certain way, our brains will likely tell us to mimic that behavior. It's a key reason why kids smoke when others smoke, why infants smile when their moms smile, and why so many of us yawn or feel impatient when someone else does. Thanks to our mirror neurons, we feel what we see. So when you see someone who needs some attention and love, those feelings tend to rise within you in an empathetic way, and you want to give attention and love to the person in front of you.

But for some people, the neurons that should fire the emotions of compassion and caring have been compromised. For example, at the outset of this chapter, I talked about my stare-down with the hulk. One thing I said to him was, "Maybe you've got a hole in your heart or a block in your brain." This was not an insult. I was describing what physically can happen in your body when caring—or any other positive emotion, for that matter—disappears or gets intercepted.

I remember working with the giant one day, his six-foot-five frame leaning forward, excited to learn. He said, "What I'd like to get to and fix today, Brendon, is why I'm so cut off. I just don't have strong emotions, man. My wife thinks it's hilarious what we're doing here, but she does hope you can make me more . . . I don't know, caring or sensitive or whatever."

His concern illustrates the reality all humans deal with. At some point in our lifetimes, we all get blocked from our emotions and the joys of experiencing and expressing greater emotional range—

including caring. Understanding how and why that happens and how to reopen the gates to an emotionally richer, more engaging and fulfilling life is what the giant had to learn.

Sometimes, it's our culture, peers, and parents who condition our beliefs about emotional expression and our patterns and feelings of worthiness about caring. But it happens more broadly than that. It's the millions of experiences we have within ourselves and the millions of interactions with others that weave the expanding tapestry of who we are and how much we care.

Two such experiences come to mind as being extremely important for you to know. Both lead to what I call "emotional brain block." One experience is about too much anxiety; the other is about too little attention.

Here's what had happened to the giant. Throughout his life, he didn't feel cared for or loved enough. Breakup after breakup and judgment after judgment left him "cut off" and "cold, detached inside," he said. What he didn't know was that this description was not just a metaphor.

When an overwhelming emotional event happens in life, your mind and brain go into protective mode. The biological process works this way: Something bad happens and your extended nervous system—your body, brain stem, limbic area, cortex—lights up immediately. Roughly speaking, emotions tend to "go vertical," rising from your body's senses to your brain stem, to the limbic area of your brain, and ultimately integrating with relevant parts of your brain, including your middle prefrontal cortex, which tells you how much conscious focus and attention to give that emotion. Of course, all this happens in a flash. And it isn't exactly a linear process, because of the vast spiderwebs of neural connectivity in the brain. But you get the gist: emotion wells up; brain decides how much attention to give it.

During times of high anxiety and stress, the mind can avoid

these sensations, effectively cutting off feeling from our subcortical regions to our prefrontal cortex so we don't have to experience the feeling as heightened conscious levels. This allows us to avoid, minimize, dampen, or "shut off" our feelings. This ability to shut down an emotion is often called a defense mechanism. And it's a good thing we have it. As we've evolved, many of the fight-or-flight emotions that make us human aren't always helpful in the moment. When you're in a meeting and someone embarrasses you, the emotions in your body say to get up and run out of the room right this second. Luckily, your mind dampens the emotion and tells you to stay put, focused on the discussion and the goal at hand.

In more dramatic trauma cases, it's also fortunate that our mind kicks in and turns our awareness away from the overwhelming sensations we're experiencing physically or emotionally. Victims of attack, rape, and physical injury often report that they were terrified but that at some point the emotions and experience changed and they "went to another place" while they were being hurt. Their minds shut down the overwhelming awareness of the situation and took them elsewhere.

That's why this defense mechanism of the mind is a blessing. But the more pain and trauma we experience, the more the pattern runs, the more the neural pathways strengthen to avoid emotion. Suddenly, we don't integrate or experience our feelings as much in our everyday lives. *And the less emotion we feel, the less care we give to ourselves and others.* Emotion, it turns out, is the spark that compels us to care in the first place.

Fortunately, we've also been given the gift of mental and emotional presence, allowing us to choose how to handle our emotions. Therapists often use this gift to help us revisit our pasts and reexperience traumatic events so that we can better manage or integrate the emotions from those times. Sometimes, they help us re-create the meaning of the experience altogether. In fact, the best therapists are those who teach their patients to manage emotion better and increase their tolerance for dealing with anxiety or negative emotion. That's why so many therapists will tell their patients to "stay with the emotion." By reengaging people with their emotions, therapists help people find a greater sense of self-care and empathy for others.

So when our friend the giant said he felt "cut off" from his emotional world, he was describing not only a feeling but also a physical tendency in how his brain operates. After all the painful breakups and judgments, he just stopped letting himself feel the pain. The neural connections that allow emotion to fire and float from our subcortex into our "front-of-the-mind" prefrontal cortex were underused. His emotional world felt flat because his neural circuits had withered.

All this has consequences beyond what most of us think. Not only do we stop feeling our emotions in general, but we also start thinking differently. Here's what was stacked up against our giant: He grew up with emotionally expressionless parents. He had been hurt enough times that he let his left brain shut down his subcortical impulses, and he stopped sensing his own emotions. His right brain's neural pathways were weakened, and his left brain started getting all the say.

Still, he managed to reach the top in his sport, spurred along by his brilliant strategies. The problem was, in his sport all his mirror neurons saw all day were men around him trying to be tough.

This all led to his sitting in front of me and seeking coaching. This was a genuinely good guy who rarely paid attention to his or others' internal worlds. He didn't feel there was any reason people should accept or love him or each other. He didn't feel like demonstrating care for others, because he never saw it, never was given the gift of it.

He, like so many people in the world, needed a new game plan.

How do we overcome the conditioning of our past? How do we

train ourselves to care more for ourselves and others, and allow others to care for us as well? How do we become a society that is more deeply kind, empathetic, caring?

As always, real change begins with real commitment to be more conscious about our goals and choices, and consistent in our efforts to make them happen. To be worthy of more caring, we simply must accept it, see that it's all around us, and, of course, return the blessing.

Like my hulk of a client, you're about to discover that putting the strategy of caring into your life can change the entire game for you.

Activator #1: Care for Thyself

Before we can receive care from others or give it freely to them, we must be congruent with our own internal drive by first caring for ourselves. Your brain and body desperately want to know that you are caring for them, looking out for the best interest of your health and overall life. When you *know* you aren't taking care of yourself, it's almost impossible to feel a sustained charge in life.

Better self-care is the foundation of all personal development. Yet in our hypersonically changing world, too many of us aren't caring for ourselves. We're so busy trying to keep up, manage everything thrown our way, and please others that we tend to care for ourselves last. That's why the majority of the general public is dehydrated, overweight, stressed-out, and sleep deprived. Yet none of these realities can be blamed on others. How much you eat, drink, balance your responsibilities, and rest is entirely up to you alone.

It's time you start caring more for yourself. You should deeply care about how you feel, what you think, what you want, what you need, and what makes you feel happy. Just as important, you should have plans and routines in place that allow you to do all these things and care for yourself in general.

Here's what I recommend:

• *Schedule a minimum of seven hours of sleep every night.* If we know anything conclusively about self-care, it's that getting a better night's sleep is the best thing you can do for your brain, body, and life. Sure, parents of newborns don't have it easy—getting just a few hours of sleep is the norm. But without exception we can all learn to manage our schedules, get some help, and find creative ways to ensure we get more sleep.

• *Remember: Smaller portions, more produce.* Your body will never feel cared for if you cram too much food down your throat or poison it with fast foods. Focus on keeping your meals to one main dish, not a big plate surrounded by other big plates. In doing so, make sure that at least a third of that plate is fresh, green produce. A green-based diet—those that are heavy in vegetables like vegetarian and vegan diets—have been proven to keep the body more nourished, more alkaline, and more free from aches, pains, and illnesses, including cancers.

• *Exercise at least three times per week.* At High Performance Academy we show how working out just three hours per week can dramatically improve overall health and brain function. If you're looking for workout advice, I would recommend that you get at least two long cardiovascular exercises in per week: one hour of a cardio-based routine and at least one shorter intense exercise per week, which would be a more anaerobic exercise like weightlifting, kettlebells, and so forth. (As always, do what's appropriate and possible for you and your current health condition, and consult your doctor when making new workout or health choices.)

- *Meditate.* Neuroscience has proven that meditation is powerful not only in reducing stress levels but also in growing new neurons and activating our capacities for more creativity, empathy, and achievement. Consider meditating twice a day, even if just for ten to twenty minutes midmorning and late afternoon. If Oprah, Russell Simmons, Jerry Seinfeld, and millions of people around the globe can find time to meditate, so can you. For a free guide to mediating effectively, visit www.TheChargeBook.com/resources.

- *Drink a* lot *more water.* You should be drinking around six liters of water per day. Not everyone agrees with me on that, which is fine, but if you maintain a healthy and active lifestyle, then six to seven isn't all that much. That means, for example, two liters by lunchtime, two liters in the afternoon, and two liters between dinner and bedtime. One of those liters should happen in the hour after your workout. Be sure to drink fresh, clean water. Give it a try. You'll be amazed at the increase in your mental and physical energy.

Let's go deeper. Another way to care for yourself is to finally give yourself a break, and a little credit. If you're like most high achievers, you're far too critical of yourself. You're too judgmental about your weaknesses and struggles in life, and you too often fail to recognize and reward yourself for a job well done. Be patient and kind to yourself. Know that the judgments you make against yourself are often the most harmful you'll ever receive.

Finally, tap into the emotional side of yourself more often. Engaging your emotions and the right side of your brain tends to fire the neurons that cause empathy. When working with the giant, I began with a request that he thought was too simple, even strange. I told him to begin consciously "checking in" to the feelings he had in his body, three different times during the day: before every meal, after a conversation (with anyone), and then again an hour before bed. I gave him these times because they're easy to remember. I advised him just to sit for a minute or two and ask, *What am I feeling right now, and why?* I asked him just to breathe in and out deeply and "feel for the feeling" and, no matter what he felt, to "stay with the feeling." He didn't have to get sucked into any emotional dramas, I told him. He just had to sit with his emotions a few times a day, as I knew it would open the flow to his right brain and ultimately his drive to care more. I also asked the giant to record a separate weekly journal entry on any and all acts of caring, kindness, and love that he witnessed and demonstrated during the week.

I knew he would think this was a hokey activity. You probably do, too. But I knew that if he did it just for a few weeks in a row, he would become more attuned to his emotional world again. In the process, he would begin strengthening or creating new neural pathways in his brain. Caring itself is a skill, and the more you do it, the better you get at it and the more it becomes an automatic mind-set and behavior.

As simple as this strategy is, you might be shocked at its results. Give it a try. Our giant suddenly found himself clearer and more connected with his emotions. He said that within two weeks, he suddenly started to feel more "grounded" and "soulful." He also said that for the first time in decades, he really felt a sense of love inside. When I asked him where that sense of love was coming from, he said, "No one said anything. I think it was just my heart breaking through my own roadblocks, breaking through, saying hello, like a long-lost friend."

Activator #2: Be More Vulnerable and
Allow Others to Care for You

Though we all want to sense that others care for us, it's remarkable how many of us have become closed to, or oblivious of, other people's expressions of emotion and caring toward us. We don't ask for help when we need it even though others have offered. We get an email asking how we've been, and we zap back a one-line response, not realizing that someone was genuinely interested in us and opening up the gate to share. We don't realize that our spouses' tidying of our houses was a sign that they love us.

Oftentimes, our awareness and receptivity to other people's caring advances has a lot to do with how we've experienced caring in the past. How attentive, attuned, and caring your parents were likely shaped your style in interacting with others. Your parents gave indications of whether they cared when you cried or needed something. This formed a basis for you to decide, *am I worthy of care and love?* It's been shown, for example, that if you grew up with attentive, attuned, and affectionate caregivers, then you tend to demonstrate those same qualities with others in your later life. The opposite is often true, too: if you received poor care when you grew up, you tend to care poorly for yourself and others. But, alas, the past is the past, and we must choose anew how we would like to live our lives.

If you don't feel "worthy" to be cared for, or you're simply "too scared to care" because in days gone by you've been hurt by opening your heart, it's time to reassess.

You are a child of God, and that alone makes you worthy of care and love. Next, regardless of your past, don't forget that allowing others to care for, give attention to, and love you is one of the greatest joys in life. If your guard is up, let it down. If you've constructed a defensive wall to protect yourself and keep all the bad guys out, don't forget who that wall also prevents from getting in—the good guys.

Being vulnerable, asking for help, allowing others in—this all requires bravery. So let's be bold and open ourselves once again to care and support from others. Here's a simple and tactical way to do that. Grab your journal and take a few moments to write down all the areas in your life that you are having challenges with. Consider all aspects of your life—your emotional, mental, social, professional, financial, and spiritual realities. What challenges or problems are you having in each area? Now, in each of these areas, write down your ultimate ambitions and dreams.

Once you've written down all your challenges and ambitions, it's time to make a decision: will you go it alone in solving these problems and fulfilling these dreams, or will you ask for help? The answer to that decision will dictate how hard and frustrating the next decade of your life will be. I say, share your results with others, ask for help, open yourself up to letting others help you, support you, mentor you, encourage you—*care for you.*

Activator #3: Be More Present, Interested, and Attentive to Others

If we can care for ourselves, and allow others to care for us, we're halfway home to activating this drive fully. The rest of our progress rests in demonstrating greater caring in the world.

"The youth of today don't need our presents; they need our presence." This was the wisdom the Reverend Jesse Jackson gave to a group of his followers on how to care for and mobilize our youth. I think this also happens to be the most relevant advice I could ever give you about relationships: impress them not with "stuff" but with your true presence.

We've become a society so caught up in the superficial that when we meet people who are truly present with us, we take notice. We can tell that they want to be here with us right now. In meetings with us, they aren't checking their phone for messages. They aren't looking around the restaurant to see who else is around who might be more important than we are. They don't seem distracted, and they're focused on the one thing we all think is most important: us.

Without question, the number one reason your relationships aren't as charged or as caring as you wish is that, frankly, you're rarely "in" the relationship. Your presence is distracted; when you're with others, you are attentive to a long list of other things besides them. Your mind is racing on tomorrow's to-do list or the thing you have to do after you get this interaction out of the way, or the words you want to say once they finally shut up talking and you finally get your turn. You're not in the moment with the other person, so he or she can't be in the moment or fully "in" the relationship with you during the interaction. The only way to experience the deepest levels of human experience is to be deeper in the moment in our interactions with others, fully invested in the now, with them alone.

Being present in our interactions with others takes tremendous focus and practice.

From now on, when anyone speaks, remind yourself: BE PRESENT. If this were the only mental reminder you give yourself in amplifying your drive to care, and in improving your relationships, and you actually thought it consistently before and during all your interactions, the caring, kindness, and love in your life would bloom.

But our presence with others should also have a goal, and that's to demonstrate that we care and want to learn something about them. Being present allows us to be curious and pay attention to others. Curiosity is really a secret to great relationships. And odds are that if you open yourself up to caring for the people around you, you'll be amazed at how much there is to know and learn and appreciate in them that you never guessed was there.

Try this simple test. Write down the ten people you interact with most frequently. The list probably includes your significant other (if you have one), coworkers, friends, and family members. Once you have this list, complete the following about each person:

- This person's top three ambitions in life are to . . .
- This person's favorite artist is . . .
- This person's three closest friends are named . . .
- This person's three best experiences in life were . . .
- This person's three worst experiences in life were . . .
- This person's favorite meal is . . .
- This person would absolutely love to own a . . .

These questions are random, of course, and, many could argue, inconsequential. But what does it say about us that we often don't know these things about those closest to us?

There is an old saying: There are two kinds of people in the world—those who walk into a room and say, "Here I am!" and those who walk into a room and say, "Oh, there you are!"

Be the second kind of person. Turn your lens to others. Ask them more questions about themselves. Be so curious about other people that they become curious about you. (That happens almost automatically, thanks to the mirror neurons in their brains.)

All of us want someone to care who we are and what we think and feel. That's why we all should see everyone in the world as having a sign hung around his neck that reads, PLEASE LISTEN TO ME AND VALUE ME. When you ask questions about someone else's reality, it's as if you've read his sign, and then, in turn, he wants to know and care more about you.

When asking questions about other people's lives, there's one question that seems to demonstrate your caring more so than others. This one approach by itself changed my life, and I am forever thankful for it. I learned the idea in an interpersonal communication class. I remember many of my fellow students liking the idea, and many of them even put it into practice for a few weeks. What's often made the difference in the quality of my life, though, is my persistence, and putting this question to the people I've met over the past fifteen years has been beyond powerful.

The strategy is simple. From now on, whenever someone shares something with you, be conscious of asking this question: "Wow, how did you feel when that happened?" Adding the word "wow" takes the you-trying-to-be-a-therapist edge off the question. (Under no circumstances should you say, "Hmmm, I see . . . Tell me how you feel about that.") Asking others this question is a gift, because it makes them pause and it shows you care about their emotions. It's also a gift to you, because it will make your interactions with others much, much deeper and more meaningful.

The happiest and most high-performing people I've met are extremely caring people. They put caring for themselves and others at the very top of their priorities in life. They demonstrate caring for others in very attentive and physical ways, and they have the guts to ask for care when they themselves need it. To them, caring is a continual life practice, not a touchy-feely concept, and because they approach this area of their lives with such a mastery mind-set, the result is a life filled with vibrant emotion. If you want to feel alive again, *care* again.

CHARGE POINTS

1. Five ways I'm going to start taking better care of myself include . . .

2. If I were willing to be more vulnerable in life, I'd probably start asking for more help in the area of . . .

3. Three ways I'll start demonstrating more care for the people in my life are to . . .

Chapter Six

THE DRIVE FOR
CONNECTION

It is well to remember that the entire population of the universe,
with one trifling exception, is composed of others.
—John Andrew Holmes Jr.

I follow Dan into his house and notice the splinters of the doorway
still preventing the door from closing fully. Glass from the portal
is strewn all about the foyer. The small console table in the hall-
way is jutting a few inches from its intended neatly aligned place
along the wall, and some of the picture frames on it are knocked
down.

Dan sees me surveying the scene and shrugs sheepishly. "We
haven't had time to clean up."

We go upstairs. Dan points to the last door on the right. I can see
splinters on the doorway there, too. "Just, uh, tell Shane I love him,
okay. Do your thing, then come find me in the kitchen whenever.
Then maybe we can get a drink?"

I nod and smile, then head to the door. This is a day when I both
hate what I do and feel honored to have developed such unique skill
sets. There's nothing harder than when your friends ask you to help
their kids.

I get to Shane's door and look in to see him sitting at his desk, writing. His mom, Rita, is sitting to his right in a chair, reading. She sees me and smiles broadly, relieved. "Shane! Look, Shane, Brendon's here!" He glances in my direction but doesn't make eye contact.

I motion to the splintered door frame and the battered door, which is barely hanging on by its bottom hinge. I know it's not funny, but sometimes just trying to break the ice shows people that you care.

"Jeez, Shane, you send a text and they send a SWAT team—break this place up like a crack house in the movies?"

Last night Shane sent a text to Nina, his former girlfriend. It said, "I have a gun. You're the reason I'm pulling the trigger. Fuck you. Fuck everyone." Nina happened to be with one of her best friends, whose father, thankfully, was a cop.

Shane just huffs and keeps his head in his homework. Rita walks over to me and gives me a hug. She looks at me hopefully, then turns to leave. "Hey, Shane, I'm just downstairs. I'll be around all day, Boogy." He doesn't acknowledge her as she leaves.

I walk around the bed, to the side of Shane's desk, and sit. I decide to wait him out. Shane writes for a minute or so and finally invites me in, though it doesn't sound like that.

"So," he says, "they sent the SWAT last night and now *you*, huh?"

"Well, I guess once they cleared out all the hos downstairs bagging the coke, they felt it was safe to send me in."

To my amazement, he smirks. I thought it would take longer.

I knew before I entered the house that I wasn't going to talk to Shane in the manner of a therapist, teacher, or concerned adult. He's sixteen years old, and teenagers have a way of talking around issues without ever really addressing them. If they do address the issue, they just skim it to watch your reaction.

"They really did the damage on these doors, man. Must have been some burly dudes."

He huffs again and doesn't look at me. But he does take aim. "They were bigger than you."

I laugh out loud. "Yeah, I bet. I don't know if I ever told you, but I tried out for the Army. They wouldn't take me because I couldn't do enough push-ups and I refused to sleep in giant rooms full of men in tighty-whities and T-shirts."

Shane lets out a genuine laugh. His dad was in the Army, so I knew he'd think this was funny. And he knows my dad was in the Marines, so I knew he'd know I was just teasing.

I'm willing to go all day talking with him this way. The best way to endear yourself to a teenager is to talk about nothing in particular, demonstrate that you're a loser or underdog, and—only when the right moment arrives—show that you give a damn.

He let's me in early. "They told you I didn't really have a gun, right?"

"No shit? Well, if those dudes were really bigger than me, I hope you had some kind of pepper spray or something."

He laughs again and, for the first time, meets my eyes. I get that teenage nod of approval that all parents dream of.

"No. I didn't have nothin'. I hear them banging on the door down there and I just didn't answer. I didn't know they'd break up in here like that."

Rule number one in moments of teenage disclosure: match their emotion and then shut up.

"I was surprised they broke in here, too."

"Yeah, what the hell? What if I did have a gun? They just would've shot me or tried to talk me down or something. But to break in here like that?"

"Sounds weird to me, too. I'm surprised. Maybe it's because they knew you or something."

Shane pauses and looks to his right, away from me, out the window.

"Well, I guess they all know now."

"Who's that?" I ask.

"Everyone. All the kids at school. I'm sure Nina told everyone. And I'm sure the cops have talked to the school and all the parents and neighborhood or whatever they do. They want me to start meeting with this therapist tomorrow, I guess."

"I'm glad they didn't throw you in jail."

"I'd rather be there, I think. How am I going to go back to school now, anyway?" He looks at me as a friend for the first time. This is a real question.

"You're just going to walk in there and be like, 'Yo, my girlfriend went nuts and called the cops and they bust up my place and I had to hustle my bag girls out the back door.'"

He laughs again, and now I know I can help.

"Or you just go in there, tell your friends you're okay, and you decide to start over. No one knows what to think of you now, but they're watching, so go show them who you want to be and who you want them to know you are."

"Yeah."

We sit for a little while and he says, "You know, I wouldn't have done it. I just got sad and I didn't feel like anyone cared. I was just mad at Nina, you know? I just wanted to scare her into caring or something. Everyone wants to know what I was thinking and why I did that. I don't know what I was thinking. I just wanted someone to connect with maybe."

By the time I get up to leave, he gives me a fist bump and one of those cool nods again. As I'm walking through his busted-up doorway, he says, "Thanks, Brendon. I know you're trying to make me feel better. I do. If I had friends like you, I wouldn't have done it."

"I know, Shane. Friendships will save your life. And despite your last experience, so will girls. Tomorrow, after your therapist meeting thing, let's go get some pizza and I'll tell you how to get a few. Sound good?"

He agrees, and downstairs when I tell Dan and Rita about all this, they break down in tears of relief. But I assure them the hard work has just begun. They're going to have to learn to connect differently with their son now. He's been to the edge. He's a different boy now.

. . .

We all want to feel connected to those around us. The challenge in our modern society is that, thanks to social media, we are more connected to more people than ever before, but those connections are more superficial than ever. In the not-too-distant past, our friendships were limited to people in our immediate neighborhoods, so pondering who our "real friends" were was a short process of elimination—we had only a handful of people to consider. Today, we have hundreds if not thousands of "friends" online. But how many of them are *real*? How many count? How many do we trust? How many could we call in times of crisis or triumph? Your friendships have as much bearing on your happiness in life as does the kind of work you do or the amount of money you make. That's why it's time you finally figured out the friendship factor in your life. This chapter will point the way.

If friendships have a big effect on your happiness, then the effects of your intimate relationships are supernovas. No other area influences your life satisfaction as much as your relationship with your spouse or significant other does. When you're in love and it's working, wow. You're giddy. You make out like teenagers and send each other stupidly cute text messages. You feel a deep emotional and spiritual connection with the one person you're supposed to be with in this moment and ever after. Nothing, and I mean nothing, provides a greater charge in life than a lit-up love life. Psychologists have found that the happiest 10 percent of people on earth have one thing in common: they all have rich, fulfilling social lives and intimate relationships.

The drive for connection—both casual and intimate—is so strong that we sometimes end up devoting time to people for much longer than they deserve. You know exactly what I'm talking about. You've been in horrible relationships and stayed too long (unless you married your high school sweetheart who actually turned out to be sweet, even into adulthood). You have strange, negative, or ambition-sucking friends you should have dumped years ago.

What could possibly spark this strange behavior? Blame it on God or evolution, but eventually both lead to one culprit: your brain. Our brains, whether divinely inspired or genetically mutated, have become tuning forks for social connection and attachment. Our desire to bond and belong outweighs almost every other desire—often even our desire for survival. Shane said he was willing to give up his life because he didn't belong or have someone to love. On the flip side, I'd give my life, too—not for lack of love but because of it. If I had to take a bullet for my wife, I wouldn't blink.

Relationship connections are like the finger on the Pez dispenser of our brains' reward areas—a good connection hits, even momentarily, and, *bam*, we get brain candy: dopamine, vasopressin, oxytocin. We feel euphoric, connected, clingy.

There's no doubt that the drive for connection has kept us alive as a species. We're less susceptible to attack and death when we hunt and stay together. We perpetuate our species when we have sex. We learn faster in social groups, advancing our abilities to outsmart our predators and master our environment. In modern times, we would have no culture, no workplaces, and no Facebook (gasp!) if we weren't so driven to share, leverage our smarts, and connect.

The problem is that as much as we want to connect with others, we also want to exert our own wills on the world and our relationships. That's where conflict comes into play—the euphoria of connecting with others often spirals into the bitterness of conflict. Naturally, we all have our individual values and viewpoints that we feel are important. When someone questions what we find important or how we see things, though, we get defensive. The more defensive we feel, the more we want to exert our independent voices, thoughts, feelings, standards. This can lead to either understanding or conflict (usually conflict, followed by understanding).

If all this is true, then perhaps our real challenge in improving our relationships across the board would be to learn to understand and communicate our own needs for independence while in interdependent relationships. Maybe we should all learn how to honor each other's individuality as we become closer to each other. After all, almost all the things that get us in trouble in our relationships—criticism, defensiveness, competition, harsh disagreements—stem from a lack of understanding, acceptance, or validation of each other's uniqueness and individuality.

That's all easier said than done, of course. But the struggle to form better, deeper, and more empowering connections and relationships is worth it. You could do everything suggested in this book, but if you fail to forge meaningful connections in life, then what's it all for? Feeling happy and energized is one thing, but being able to share that energy and enthusiasm with others you deeply care about and adore is the real hallmark of a fully Charged Life. True lifelong happiness comes from connecting with and loving others, so it's best we figure out how to do that as soon as possible and as best we can. The strategies below will help you do just that.

Activator #1: Define and Design Your Ideal Relationships

Surprisingly, few people have ever paused long enough in life to ask themselves, *What exactly do I want in my relationships in life?*

What kinds of friends do I want, exactly? What kinds of lovers do I want? And how shall I attract, keep, and deepen my relationships with them?

But these kinds of questions are exactly what Chargers ask themselves. They're consciously designing their lives *and* all the relationships within them to the highest degree possible.

Amplifying your own relationships with others begins by defining what your ideal relationships look like, and then designing your behaviors and interactions to make them a reality. This is important work, because the more you feel you are in your ideal relationships, the more your drive for deep, meaningful connections is satiated.

There are four types of relationships we'll work on in this section: family, friends, lovers, and peers/coworkers. (We'll leave the fifth type of relationships—acquaintences—out for now, as the greatest levels of connection and joy have been shown to come from the prior four.)

To begin, please grab your journal or your computer, as I'm going to ask you to do some thinking and writing before proceeding. Please answer the following questions:

i. What defines a happy and deeply connected family relationship to you?

What would you have to do to improve and deepen the relationships you have with the people in this area?

ii. What defines a happy and deeply connected friendship to you?

What would you have to do to improve and deepen the relationships you have with the people in this area?

iii. What defines a happy and deeply connected intimate relationship to you?

What would you have to do to improve and deepen the relationships you have with the people in this area?

iv. What defines a happy and deeply connected peer/ coworker relationship to you?

What would you have to do to improve and deepen the relationships you have with the people in this area?

I'm always asking myself and my clients questions like these. I ask you the same because it's important for you to begin with the end in mind in your relationships—to define what you want and to endeavor to bring it into existence. As simple as the activity is, it can lead to profoundly powerful results if you take it seriously.

I did this same activity with Shane, the boy from the beginning of the chapter. When I asked what would make a happy family life, he said it would be defined by a high degree of fun, authenticity, sharing, optimism, enthusiastic support, and willingness from his parents to allow him to take risks and have new experiences. He allowed me to share this with his parents, and they were surprised—not at his description per se, but about how unaware and lacking they felt in making his ideal family life a reality. They realized that as Shane had entered his teenage years and started to express more independence, they also stopped planning fun family outings and adventures. They expressed interest in his school life, but not enthusiastic support for who he was becoming. The list went on. Ultimately, being aware of Shane's list helped them become better parents.

In discussing friends, Shane said he wanted friends who were more engaged and curious about life outside of their community. He wanted to have friendships defined by more sharing and adventure. I asked if he'd be willing to share that with the few friends he did have and if he could start new friendships with those two things in mind. He got it, and for the first year after we worked together, he reminded himself to be "the curious kid" at school. He joined a few student groups, sought friends who had similar passions and hobbies as he, asked to be mentored by two of his teachers, and started mentoring students in grades below his own. He went on to form some great friendships at school and became a genuinely interested and happy man.

This leads me to this—you should consider sharing with others what your ideal relationships with them would look like. If they know, they are more empowered to connect better with you. Of course, you should also ask them what their ideal realtionships with you would look like.

It's such a simple thing: ask others what they desire from us in relationship, and share ours with them as well. Yet we often forget to do it. I remember once asking my mother what would help her feel more connected to me, her middle son. She said, "You'd have to call me every Sunday and just talk with me and tell me you love me." I started doing that and have done so for almost fifteen years.

There are two ways to deepen the connections you have with people in your life: one is by accident as you're brought closer by tragedy or chance; one is by design. If you're willing to do the hard work of defining and sharing what you want, and you're willing to listen to and meet others' desires as well, you'll find that all of your relationships grow. Be clear about what you want and what others want, and work to create relationships that you're both proud of. Do this for life, and you'll find yourself with happy and healthy lifelong relationships.

Activator #2. Practice Positive Projection

Great teachers and great married couples know something in common. If they want the best from their students or their spouses, they must see the best in them and expect the best from them. This is the mightiest of all social truths: *you get what you look for.* If you project positive traits and expectations onto others, not only do you notice those positive traits more often, but people also tend to live up to them.

The challenge is, too many of us are too guarded or cynical. We've been hurt before, so the three-pound anticipation machine in our skulls starts looking for trouble. People's faults become the focus of our social scanning. The logic makes sense: if I can find out what is wrong with someone as quickly as possible, then I can more quickly avoid pain from him or her. Over time, we stop seeing people's strengths and see only their weaknesses or behaviors that might bother or hurt us.

And that's just our personal social filter at work, based on our own experience of pain in the past. Add to this the overwhelmingly cynical and critical societal context we live in, and it's amazing that we connect with anyone. Our negative society has taught us to look for (and comment on) the negative in one another. Media outlets survive on how many "gotcha" moments they can capture with politicians and celebrities. *Breaking news: this person is a liar. Breaking news: this person is a cheat. Breaking news: this person said something stupid. Breaking news: she looked fat in that dress.* This "gotcha" journalism has only thickened our social filter's looking for the bad traits, big mistakes, and superficial faults of others.

Viewing the world through a negative lens has more tragic consequences than you could possibly fathom. Take, for example, the famous expectation studies in which one set of children is told they are smart and capable, and the other set is told they are not. Guess which group performs better? Guess which group feels better about itself? Guess which group goes further in life? Guess which group reports being happier decades later. That's right: the group that was given the gift of "positive projection." Any teacher in the world would report the same thing: the more positives we see and project onto our students, the more they "live into" that expectation.

This concept doesn't apply just to children. Researchers have found that the happiest married couples in the world see each other as smarter, more capable, more caring, and more filled with goodwill than their behavior might demonstrate. Happy couples make more excuses for each other's bad behavior or shortcomings. *Oh, he was just tired; he didn't really mean it. She usually doesn't act like that in social settings; she must have been distracted.* These excuses come from the fact that they see their lovers in a universally positive light.

This all might seem like turning a blind eye to reality or doing a silly optimistic override of the truth, but here's the rub: these kids and these couples *are happier* and more likely to live into the positive truth simply because they are expected to. When people are told that they are usually attentive, charming, and pleasant, they themselves will start behaving that way; they will see the tired or distracted behavior as anomalous rather than a rule about who they are. When you live your life believing that people are generally good and interesting, you will find the good and interesting aspects of every person you interact with.

Carrying the torch of optimism into your social relationships is probably the best thing you could ever do to start feeling better about humanity. If you see people as smart, caring, interesting, and helpful, they tend to show up that way. So project positive traits onto others, and let them *live into* those traits.

One of the most powerful results of positive projection is that you stop seeing others as obstacles or competitors and instead see them as teammates or valued opponents on the road of life. These distinctions are critical to all your connections in life. If storms or opportunities arise and you perceive others as obstacles to your safety or success, you will avoid them, push them aside, and act outside your kind character and virtue. But if you consider them teammates, you wonder how you can face the storm or charge for success *together*. You leverage one another's success and skills, and you get further together than you could by yourself. Also, note the important distinction between seeing someone as a competitor and seeing him as an opponent. When you cast someone in the negative light of "competitor," you immediately see him as an obstacle to your achieving what you want. You inject scarcity into your view of others. But when you see someone as a worthy opponent, you recognize his strengths and understand that it is those very strengths that will help you and challenge you to engage your own strengths.

To project positively onto others requires that, at some level, we make an *assumption* about them and about humans in general. You must assume they are good, capable, well intentioned. What would happen if you started assuming the people in your life were brilliant, caring, worthy, and on their own wondrous journeys to achieve their dreams? If you saw others this way, what would happen to your interactions with them?

Of course, seeing others haloed in a positive glow of goodness is not easy. It requires you to abstain from judging others quickly and that you take the time to really engage and connect with people even if you initially suspect that you don't have any common ground. It requires you to acknowledge and honor their uniqueness. It requires you to see the best in them and believe that goodness and humanity are part of who they are, part of their character. In short, it requires love.

Naturally, conflict happens, and it's hard to always positively project the best upon our loved ones, so here's a parting study for you to consider. Marriage researchers have found a powerful equation you should be aware of. Happily married couples who end up staying together for life have in common the ratio in which they share positive versus negative input. That ratio is five to one. So you should aspire to give five times as much praise in your relationships as criticism. Be the cheerleader, not the cynic. Coupled together, your intention to positively project onto others and also praise them five times more than complain will change your relationships forever.

Activator #3: Find and Cultivate "Growth Friends"

People worldwide report that their family and intimate relationships are the primary source of their feelings of connection and love. The secondary source comes from our friendships, so it's worthwhile to think how you can activate greater friendships in your life.

To my continual surprise, most people don't have a real grasp on how vital their friendships are to their overall mental health and happiness. In study after study, researchers from a variety of disciplines continually find that the quality of our immediate friendship-based relationships is one of the most important factors in determining our overall stability, mood, ambition, emotional range, growth, and satisfaction in life.

In our friendships, it's useful to heed this warning: Be careful whom you surround yourself with. While that counsel seems like kitchen-table wisdom, you'd be surprised by who most people invite to their tables of friendship. You'd also be surprised how many people barely invite anyone to their tables. The average American has only one or two close friends. That's unfortunate, but it does give us a ready clue to how they can immediately increase their life satisfaction.

Let's take a look at your own peer group. Answer the following questions:

1. How many close, real friends do you have? (You alone can define "close" and "real" for yourself.)
2. How often do you see them in person?
3. How often do you speak with them?
4. On a scale of one to five, with one being the lowest amount possible, how well do these close friends really know you?
5. On a scale of one to five, with one being the lowest amount possible, how much do these close friends consistently encourage you to chase your dreams?

6. On a scale of one to five, with one being the lowest amount possible, how much do these close friends provide you with insight, information, and inspiration that challenge you to be a better person?

7. On a scale of one to five, with one being the lowest amount possible, how much fun do you have when you hang out with these close friends?

With these questions and your answers, you can clearly discover a lot about yourself and your immediate circle of friends. You can also gauge how supported, understood, connected, and enlivened you feel in your friendships. It's hard to take on people's friendships, but this is territory we must venture into together if we are to achieve a new level of living.

Without sugarcoating, here are the responses you're going to need to live a fully Charged Life:

1. Four to twelve
2. You must see them, or at least one of them, in person every month.
3. You must speak to them, preferably several of them, every week or two at a minimum.
4. Five
5. Five
6. Five
7. Five

If my suggestions here sound unattainable to you, as your coach, I must be blunt: your life is in very serious need of rethinking.

As a society, many of us spend more time picking the style and thread count of bedsheets we'll use in our homes than picking our friends. By default, then, we have family, friends, coworkers, and peers who are thrust into our lives. We cannot always choose these people. But we can choose two things: how much time we give them, and how much energy we expend seeking to expand the circle and quality of such relationships.

The old adage is true: You can't choose family, but you can choose friends. Now it's time to take that to heart. Strategically make the choice today to start surrounding yourself with remarkable friends who help lift your life to the level of energy and potential you know it has.

To help you do this, I'm going to ask you to make some tough choices about whom to spend your time with from now on. I'll warn you in advance, doing so won't be comfortable.

Let's face it: there may be a few friends in your life who aren't adding to the quality and desired direction in your life. It sounds like a horribly judgmental and selfish thing to say, I know. And while it seems to counter what I've said about connecting with others—that we must accept them and see them for the positive gifts they are— the truth is, we can develop deep relationships with only so many people in our lives. If that's true, we have to face the fact that we're better off spending our time with some people than with others. All those people we might be in a habit of calling or connecting with might not really be contributing to our life experiences and happiness. There are battery chargers and there are battery drainers, and there are those with no charge whatever—the "neutrals." To live a fully Charged Life, we've got to get real about who those people are.

At High Performance Academy, one of my most controversial strategies is helping people do just that: get real about the people in their lives. Specifically, I have people focus on categorizing their friendships and finding which friends in life they're going to develop deeper relationships with. In doing so, people are forced to select those they will no longer spend as much time with.

That's why the activity meets with so much indecision and

resistance. But after it's over, people continually share with me that it ends up being one of the most powerful strategies they put into their lives to feel more alive and connected. Because of those results, I'm sharing the strategy here with you, even if it brings temporary discomfort.

Let's begin. In your journal or on a piece of paper, please write down the names of all the friends you've had in life, one name per line. This includes elementary school friends and those from high school, college, work, sports, and your hobbies.

Next, write a short description of (a) what about them made you choose them and like them as friends, and (b) why you are still, or are no longer, friends with them.

Inevitably, this exercise brings to mind many old friends we've forgotten about or fallen out of touch with. That's okay. Part of the benefit of this activity may be to reengage with some old friends.

Now that you've got your list of friends, it's time to categorize them into one of three buckets: old friends, maintenance friends, and growth friends.

Those in the first bucket, old friends, are just that: dated, stale. These are people who were once your friends in the past, whom you no longer wish to keep in contact with. Importantly, though, you may decide to lump some of your *current* friends into this bucket. I say this because I imagine there are some friends in your current life whom you don't really want to hang out with anymore and whom you don't see having starring roles in your future. Hard though it may be, at some point we must decide whom we keep on the stage of friendship in our lives. From now on, anyone you mark as "old friends" will be left where they belong, in the past. These will be people you appreciate in your mind and memories forever, but they simply won't play important roles in your future. The second bucket is called "maintenance friends," because these are the relationships you will now maintain for the rest of your life. Maintenance friends are those you've appreciated having in your life and still want to keep up with from time to time. These are the people to whom you still send holiday or birthday cards, letters, or emails a few times a year. Perhaps you call them randomly a few times a year just to "see how it's going." Please mark "maintenance friends" next to those who fit this description.

For far too many of us, maintenance friends become mental drags in our lives because every time we think of them, we say to ourselves, *Gosh, I should really keep in better contact with this person.* But let's be honest—if you aren't keeping in more regular contact with these folks, it's because (a) you really don't feel that close to them, (b) you simply don't see them adding that much joy to your life, (c) you don't see them in your future, or (d) you keep blaming not having enough time as the problem, when the real culprit is you just don't highly prioritize these folks. If that's true, it's time to make the difficult decision once and for all to designate them as mainte-nance friends and *be okay* with just contacting them a few times a year to stay in touch. I view maintenance friends not as "bad friends" but simply as friends I'd like to say hello to now and then and see how they're doing. I will always keep up with them, but I won't focus on creating deeper levels of contact and friendship with them. So . . . from today forward, no more guilt about maintenance friends. Keep in your mental file that they are maintenance friends, and take joy in the few times you contact them, like during birthdays and holidays.

This is not an exorcism or an excommunication. Offending, brushing off, or dumping old friends and maintenance friends because they don't meet some new criteria is not the message here. Many self-help authors make all-too-casual suggestions for you to ditch any negative people in your life, treating them as if they were of no more consequence than a side salad you didn't order. To gain new things in life, you don't have to burn bridges with the old, no matter how easy and convenient it might be.

Personally, I feel that too many people take their friends for granted, forget who their friends are, or never give enough of themselves to their friendship circles to receive anything back. So by no means am I telling you to destroy any relationships you've built. The universe has likely placed each of your current friends in your path for reasons known or unknown to you. Honor that and honor them, no matter what direction you decide to go in the future.

With all my clients, my first point of advice isn't to dump their friends; it's first to try to raise them up. I suggest you reengage your close friends and, by sharing your vision for a bigger future and by sheer role modeling and enthusiasm, you be the catalyst that raises the standards and quality of your friendships. Remember, there are two things that change your life: either something new comes into life, or something new comes out of you.

Before pushing old friends away, I encourage you to sit down with your friends and authentically and excitedly share—perhaps for the first time ever—your true thoughts, feelings, and ambitions in life and for your immediate and distant future. Friendships are really only built by sharing such things and by reliving stories and creating new stories together.

That said, I do understand that this effort will fail with some of your current friends. The tough call afterward is that for your future quality of life there will be people to whom you will need to limit your duration and frequency of exposure. The sad truth is, the world is full of bitter, complaining, finger-pointing energy vampires who suck all the joy and ambition out of life. Give them a shot at coming into the light, but if they won't, steer as clear of them as you can.

Here's the best strategy in this case: if you're not getting the quality of friendship you need from one peer group, go build a new one and focus more of your time, energy, and sharing there. From now on, be on the lookout for remarkable people whose path the universe has allowed to intersect with yours. Notice them. Ask them to lunch. Keep in touch. Introduce them to other remarkable people. Have them share real thoughts, feelings, and ambitions in life. Get them together often for new adventures and experiences. This is the path to cultivating real relationships that keep your life engaging and satisfying.

Alas, the focal point of your life should now turn toward finding and cultivating what I call "growth friends." As labeled, these are the people you are actively going to engage with, grow with, and energize your life with. To me, growth friends are those you talk to at least once a month, if not more. They're the ones you go out with on the weekends or on big new adventures: trips to new cities or countries, weekend getaways. Growth friends are supremely important to your mental health and spiritual energy in life. These are the people who become your closest confidants, your partners in adventure, your godparents of your children.

My goal for your growth-friend category is to get it up to a minimum of ten. Obviously, friendships are about quality, not quantity, yet having more growth friends *will* add the increased novelty and connection needed to amp up your life. Many people tell me they already have ten close friends, but when I ask the following questions they realize they don't:

- Is this a friend you're excited to speak with every week or every month?
- Is this a friend you see being an important part of your exciting future?
- Is this a friend who would drop everything to come support you in crisis?
- Is this a friend *you* would drop everything for to support in crisis?
- Is this a friend you are excited to have know your family and friends now and in the future?

- Is this a friend who exposes you to new ideas and adventures?
- Is this a friend who is good for your long-term health?
- Is this a friend who makes you laugh a lot?
- Is this a friend who cares about your emotions, well-being, and happiness?
- Is this a friend you can trust, no matter what, with anything?
- Is this a friend who introduces you to other quality people?

Positive answers to all these questions indicate that you have a growth friend.

If you think having ten growth friends is too many or too hard, I sympathize. But you're blessed to walk the planet for, on average, sixty to eighty *years*. You can't create just ten deep, lasting, energizing friendships? What else in life is it you're so focused on creating?

Having a group of at least ten awesome friends should be in the top five goals of every human being. The zest, energy, and connection that comes with having great friends is incalculable and indescribable. Every happy person I've ever met had deep connections with multiple friends. If you're not already there, the time to begin is now. Fun, fulfilling friendships amplify your life energy—they're one of the greatest ingredients to a fully Charged Life.

One last thought. The way to cultivate growth friends is to *be one*. Role-model the types of relationships you want in life. You want love? Then be a supremely loving human being and you will find and feel love. You want real friendship? Be a passionately interested friend who brings novelty, joy, caring, adventure, and closeness to others.

As with all the things we desire in life, I believe we can have them. It simply takes focus and consistent effort. You deserve to have deep, caring, fully engaged relationships with those around you.

CHARGE POINTS

1. Five things I could do immediately to create happier and deeper relationships in my life would be . . .

2. If I did a better job in positively projecting toward my spouse or significant other, I would start to give that person credit for these things . . .

3. The growth friends I have in my life or will now cultivate include . . .

THE FIVE
FORWARD DRIVES

CHANGE

CHALLENGE

CREATIVE EXPRESSION

CONTRIBUTION

CONSCIOUSNESS

Chapter Seven

INTRODUCING THE FORWARD DRIVES

Our purpose is to consciously, deliberately evolve towards a
wiser, more liberated and luminous state of being.
—TOM ROBBINS

The five baseline drives we've covered so far—control, competence, congruence, caring, and connection—and how we activate them clearly influence the quality and energy of our lives. When
we feel out of control, incapable of figuring things out, incongruent,
uncared for, and disconnected or distant from others, our lives are
miserable. But when we feel in command of our own lives, capable
of learning and understanding our world, in integrity with who we
think we are and how we behave, cared for, and in touch with our
hearts and the hearts of others, we start to feel a distinctly heightened and even positive charge in our lives. Activating these baseline
drives helps us meet many of our basic biological needs for stability
and love, and they certainly help us feel more in touch with ourselves
and others. In this way, I think of the baseline needs as critical to the
sanity and development of our sense of self and social belonging.
Stable, secure, socially connected. That's a great recipe for comfort
and happiness in life.

But there's more to life than feeling comfortable or happy. We're after feeling charged and fulfilled, and to get there, we'll have to raise our ambitions and take on a whole other level of human drive and motivation—the forward drives. The baseline drives get you in the game of living a fully Charged Life, but it's the forward drives that lead to the home runs. They cause you to swing at bigger aspirations in life, from feeling more creatively engaged to experiencing emotional transcendence.

Before I jump into the forward drives, I want to emphasize that they aren't truly separate from the baseline drives, or necessarily hierarchically stacked on top of them. While separating all our human drives provides clarity and structure for this book, we must remember that these drives are always at play in our minds, jockeying and vying for control of our attention and activation. Everything is connected. Our drive for control, for instance, dramatically affects how we activate our drive for change (the first forward drive and the topic of the next chapter). It's hard to take on change in our lives, because we don't want to feel out of control. With this in mind, it's important to know that the level in which we learn to master our baseline drives dramatically affects our ability to activate our forward drives. So make sure you've read the previous chapters, taken notes, and begun taking action.

The five forward drives, which I'll call "f-drives" from here on, are: Change, Challenge, Creative Expression, Contribution, and Consciousness. There are a few things you should know about these drives that make them distinct and more challenging to master than the baseline drives.

First, while the baseline drives make you feel more secure and stable, the f-drives function to *shake you up* so that you can ultimately feel more satisfied. The f-drives are simply harder and more uncomfortable to fully activate on a consistent basis. Because of this, there is a *lot more resistance* to activating the f-drives. It's relatively easy to convince people to want more caring and connection in their lives, for instance, but it's a whole lot harder to persuade them to take on more change and challenge. People already feel they're struggling under the tidal wave of change and challenge in their lives, so why would they want more? That's what you'll discover in coming chapters, and that foreshadows how hard our work will get from here forward.

Second, the f-drives are more *future oriented* than the baseline drives, many of which we automatically or unconsciously seek to activate on a daily basis. It's easy and almost automatic for most of us to control our thoughts in the moment, learn something new, live with congruity, care for someone in need, and connect with someone around us. But to move our lives by leaps and bounds with these f-drives, we have to *plan*. For example, when thinking about the contributions we want to make in our lives, we have to be very thoughtful about our lives and legacies in the future. It takes a lot of vision, too, to figure out what to change in our lives and what challenges we'll take on next month and next year. This work, though, is what makes the f-drives so engaging and exciting—looking to our future and dreaming big creates enthusiasm, one of the hallmark feelings of a Charged Life.

Finally, the f-drives demand boldness. Incremental change isn't going to create giant leaps in your life satisfaction. It just won't. To fully activate the f-drives, you'll have to demand more of yourself and take bolder actions than you may ever have before. You'll have to blast through thoughts of impossibility, rise above petty concerns about rejection, and even transcend your own consciousness to connect with something larger than yourself. This will be some of the most important work of your life. And it will be worth it.

Change kicks off these more future-oriented and fulfilling drives. Human beings have an insatiable desire for newness and variety, and to get them, we often have to change ourselves or our world. We all believe the grass is greener on the other side of the fence, and the lengths we go to catapult ourselves over that fence are nothing short of awesome. But chasing change simply for change's sake is as dangerous as it is thrilling. When we manage our desire for change intelligently and strategically, on the other hand, we get all the benefits of a novel and ever-changing quality of life. On the flip side, if we're always trying to activate the Pez dispenser in our minds that hits us with quick drops of the novelty-loving dopamine hormone, we quickly get burned out or addicted to meaningless change. Too much change and we're freaked out; too little and we're bored. Learning the balance and learning why so many of us fear change is the conversation in chapter 8.

The most powerful drive for advancing our lives—and what I'm convinced is the secret and most important ingredient of a Charged Life—is *challenge*. That's because it is in times of challenge that we are most engaged. Whether challenge is self-imposed or imposed on us by the world, it forces us to give our full attention, leverage our strengths, stretch our limits, learn, and grow. When engaged in a challenge, we lose our sense of time and, to some extent, ourselves. It's why you look up from playing a video game, painting a picture, writing a book, or going a few rounds on the mechanical bull, and suddenly it's hours later. Challenge is really the great unifier of all the drives in that it introduces a change in our lives that we must now control, build new competence around, and, often, socially manage (activating caring and connection). The challenge—er, problem— with challenge is that it's scary, so most people avoid it, preferring instead to set and work toward "smart" goals. You'll learn the difference between goals and challenges—and get a good kick in the butt—in chapter 9.

Creative expression is the grand driver and amplifier of satisfaction in life. When we feel we are expressing our unique selves consistently, we feel truly alive and energized. But take away our creativity, and we slowly start to feel as though we're just another cog in the wheel of a lifeless, impersonal world. This drive is what makes you want to draw, play an instrument, dance, write, sing, design, debate, dress up, invent, build, and tell stories. It's why you spend hours trying on new clothing, searching for the perfect quote to share on Twitter, and walking multiple laps around Pottery Barn. Creative expression is the most significant shaper of "self," letting us define and differentiate who we are within our own minds and within the context of our social world. Unfortunately, most people don't actually see themselves as creative and lack an appreciation for just how vital creativity is to succeeding in today's modern workforce and global economy. Hopefully, you won't fail the Creative Expression Quiz in chapter 10.

What we give to the world is how we gauge our place in the world and whether we ever mattered, so the drive for *contribution* is a vitally important desire to understand and activate. If you feel that you are contributing authentic and significant value to the world, you feel the satisfaction of pride and fulfillment. You feel as though you count and have made your mark. But what will your *real* contribution be? And does contribution have to be some big kind of financial gift or grand legacy that you leave? What kinds of contributions make us feel the most alive? The answers in chapter 11 might surprise you.

The most difficult drive to tackle is the drive for heightened *consciousness*. At our deepest core and in our loftiest ambitions, we desire to transcend ourselves and connect with something greater. We want to experience a deeper sense of knowing about our reality and relationships with others, the universe, perhaps God. This drive makes us seekers of meaning, self-actualization, and spirituality, or connection with oneness. It also makes us weird, often seeking meaning in inanimate objects or starting wars to defend something we've never seen or been able to explain fully. How do we tap into this drive that makes us so uniquely human? What levels of transcendence exist for us, and can we reach them without wearing Birkenstocks or sitting in a full lotus? We'll see in chapter 12.

These forward drives are clearly higher-order drives than the first five, but they're all important. Can you imagine *not* activating one of these drives well in your life? Remove any one of them, and your happiness equation in life falls to pieces. Understanding and mastering all 10 human drives seems daunting, but the good news is that taking on daunting challenges is one of the surest ways to feel alive once again.

Chapter Eight

THE DRIVE FOR
CHANGE

When you're through changing, you're through.

—Bruce Barton

I can't get myself to change, and it's destroying my life."

The man sitting next to me at the airport makes his living telling companies how to change their entire technology infrastructures. He apparently swoops into global corporations with a small team and gets their tens of thousands of employees to adopt newer and more complex software and systems. It's all a bit over my head, but I feel at home since this is a very common situation in my life: I meet someone new, ask him a few questions about his life, and within minutes he's telling me, with surprising openness, what he does, what makes him happy, and what prevents him from living his dream life.

At first, I think this guy has it all together. But then I ask, "Are there any areas of your life that you're unhappy with, that are preventing you from living the life you want?"

He shrugs, then with a surprising degree of nonchalance says, "I can get ten thousand employees to completely change the way they do work, through newer and more complex technologies. But I can't even change my friggin' diet. I just keep packing on the fat and sticking to the same old same old, my wife keeps getting unhappier day by day, and, frankly, if I don't change everything, I know I'll end up bored, alone, and miserable. So there you go, man." He looks at me, and I see defeat in his eyes. "I'm a smart guy," he says. "I've tried to make a plan and stick to it, but nothing works. I honestly have no idea how to change my life and make it stick. For me, change is a real bitch."

It's not that he doesn't intellectually understand the process for making change happen. He probably does—that's how he can get people to adopt a new system. But when we're off the clock and not being paid to adopt new systems and changes, it's a whole different ball game. It doesn't take long to realize that this guy's problem isn't just congruence; it's a lack of understanding of his own drive for change.

I won't play sympathizer, even with strangers. I bring the sword in life and the battle call of challenge to live our highest, boldest, most engaged selves. What this man is saying to me stokes the flame in my gut to push him.

"So you're fat. Your life is boring. Your wife is pissed." I smile as I hear him laugh; then I drop the hammer. "And yet you're telling me you're a smart guy? What's that about?"

I pause as I say this last bit, and I fix my eyes squarely on his for a purposely uncomfortable time. I'm going after his fight-or-flight mechanism.

He shakes his head and doesn't know how to take this. "Well, yeah. Uh, jeez, man, I'm just sayin . . ."

I smile to give him relief, but I lean in close, as if I'm going to reveal a secret. "Look, I'm just a random dude you met in an airport, and I realize what I'm about to say to you might not be nice. But I bet what I'm about to say makes me nothing but a third-party mouthpiece for your own internal voice. Here it is, man: You're *not* being smart. If you were, you'd focus on your health, life, and wife as much as you do on mastering your work. If you were really driving your attention and your will at these changes you want to make, you would conquer. I can tell you're a high performer and a badass. There's a bolder man inside you than the one sitting next to me now."

I wouldn't have said this to him if I didn't think I could get away with it and if it weren't true. I don't take change casually, nor do I take fate casually, and that is what brought him and me together in this moment.

He reacts as I thought he would. He sits up, shakes his head in acknowledgment. "You're right. You're right."

"I know. So let's get smart together for a moment. These big change programs you tell me you implement to get people to adopt your systems stuff. How big are those changes?"

"Oh, they're massive. Complete changes."

"Got it. And how well researched and planned out are those changes?"

"They're completely researched and planned out. We plan everything. We have more work plans and spreadsheets and PowerPoints than you can imagine. Our resources are immense. We even write emails for executives to send out to their people along the way."

"Got it. And how long does it take to make this change? You do it, what, in a month or two?"

"No, no. It takes on average eight to ten months to make it all happen. And that's fast. It used to take us eighteen."

I stare at him with my best "you dumbass" look.

He gets it. "Man. I hear what you're saying. Complete change. Completely planned out. Work it hard. I've got to approach my personal life in a different way. That's what you're saying."

"Right. Just like at work, where you swing at the fences with big change, you've got to swing at the fences for a radical health change. Screw this crap you see in the media about making small changes.

Eating a few less Doritos ain't gonna get you fit and vibrant. You're smarter and stronger and more dedicated than you've been showing up in the world, with your health and probably with everyone in your life. You got more in you."

I see resolve light in his eyes. I'm not just stoking this guy's ambition to make my airport layover more exciting. I know that this guy, like most of us, won't do a damn thing unless he has *fire* in his gut to make real changes.

"*Damn*. I don't know what I've been doing."

I swat him on the shoulder and nod with approval and fire in my eyes. "Doesn't matter. You know what to do. Go home and get your health on track. Go home and rock your wife's world. Go home and change for her and light her up. Change into the man you can be."

．　．　．

We all know we need to change in some areas of our lives. But so many of us are awash in the jetstream of continual change in life that we rarely want to deal with any more change. Our internal drive, though, demands that we must.

The drive for change stems not only from our biological call to grow and learn but also from our conscious and continual desire for newness and excitement. Our bodies' cells demand that we change, and our brains demand that we learn and keep engaged and entertained. Unlike the five baseline drives—for control, competence, congruence, caring, and connection—which stem more from our biological need for stability, self-knowledge, and love, the drive for change is of a different sort. It is of a higher conscious order than the others, demanding more processing power in the front of our brains and more forward-looking vision from our minds. That's why it's so hard to do, but that's also why it's so powerful in helping us move boldly and determinedly into the future—thus, it is the first of the forward drives.

146

At a collective level, it would seem we've really mastered the human drive for change. The drive in our society seems to have expanded like the universe, at warp speed and by orders of magnitude that few can even comprehend. For better or worse, we have evolved into change junkies. The striving to change our lot, to grow and expand, has led to many of our greatest human accomplishments: art, architecture, agriculture, Apple. It has also led us to overdevelop, start wars over territories that did not belong to us, and seek to conquer and consume everything in our path. Change is not necessarily progress, but no one can doubt our culture is changing at the speed of light.

Individually, though, we find change difficult. This is odd, since change has been our constant companion and friend in progress throughout life. We crawled, we walked, and then we ran. We changed from barely two feet long as babies to five or six feet tall as adults. Our brains and bodies have built and blasted through trillions of cells. The air in our lungs, the sounds in our ears, the images in our eyes, the thoughts in our heads, and the sensations in our bodies have all constantly changed, every instant of every day of our entire existence. Our life experience and wisdom has broadened with every new effort, interaction, failure, and success. Our values have changed; our behavior has changed; our dreams have changed. In a broader social context, it seems that every single day a new innovation disrupts the very world we know so well. We walk into work, and there's a new project to begin or system to manage or new hire to get to know. We come home and hear that the same has happened at our spouse's work, and we struggle to talk about it while the kids play with some new game-changing gadget. We turn on the news, and the world is rocked by new scandals, new crises, new dramas, and new celebrities to obsess about. We walk into our favorite shopping mall, and everywhere we look is New! New! New!

We should be used to this. But many people do not see or sense

its magic or permanence in their lives. They see it as an intermittent thing, a pestilent thing that rears its troublesome head at the worst of times, an unexpected interruption of certainty. This view sees change as disruptive, and for that it must be feared, avoided, or tamed. How can this be? How can something that we are so familiar with, something we so thoroughly and intimately know, cause so many people such stress? Why do so many of us bathe change in fear?

As with all human drives, the answer has a lot to do with how we have thought about and activated change in our lives in our past. Regardless of the past, though, I believe that you can gauge your chances of living your dream life from today forward by the answer to this simple question: *Do I both welcome and cause change?* If the answer is yes, you can smoothly navigate the flow of life and reach your desired end. If the answer is no, you will always feel tossed about and terrified by a turbulent stream of chance, and you will live life grasping at any certain shore that appears before you.

If you get a handle on anything in life this year, get a handle on how you feel about, leverage, and drive change. Doing so will make you feel more stable yet excited, more blessed yet determined. You must know this—change is the only path to your dreams, because to grasp them, you must move from here to there. Here are the activators to make that journey even more enjoyable.

Activator #1: Make Change About the Gains, Not the Losses

It's important to reshape how you may be thinking about change, because so many people fear it that they simply suppress the drive. But doing so is catastrophic. When we stop activating the drive to change, life feels the opposite of expansive or exciting; it feels small, stagnant, boring. We feel "okay" about life, but with no changes to look forward to, we feel blasé. We wonder where our hunger and ambitions went. We sleep fine at night, but we miss the nights we

used to lie awake dreaming of a bigger, bolder, brighter future. And if we ever do dream at night, we let our dreams die in the daylight, because we've lost the guts to make the necessary changes in our lives to go from here to there.

There are thousands of reasons why you might fear change and see it as a painful thing to be avoided at all costs. Maybe someone in your life died and thrust unwanted change on you too quickly. Maybe every time you got comfortable, the world threw you a curveball of crap for some reason. Maybe you never got what you wanted whenever you tried to make a change yourself. Maybe you're just fearful of breaking routine or being judged. Some people even argue that you may fear change out of some biological programming.

I've activated change in people's lives professionally for more than a decade, though, and I've come to realize this: People don't fear change at all; in fact, most people even consciously pull for change. Rather, people fear what change will or won't bring. Thus, it is in *expectation* that the demon of fear really resides.

It's a no-brainer that some of us have linked up in our minds that change equals pain. But the subtle part of what I've learned is that it's the expectation of three specific kinds of pain that makes us fear change. The first reason has to do with an *expectation of loss*. You imagine the upcoming change taking control of your life and stripping from you something you enjoy, love, or are comfortable with. You fixate on all the things you will lose once you make or experience the change. And because you expect to lose more than you gain, you become fearful, or unmotivated.

For example, say your boss announces that your position has changed and you're being transferred to a new department. You can meet this news with any of three main emotions: curiosity, optimism, or fear of loss. If it's fear, you focus intently on losing your nice office, losing the power you worked so hard to attain in this department, losing the chance to work with your favorite coworkers, losing the certainty of knowing what you're supposed to do with your day. This expectation of loss is where all the damage is done.

Of course, bystanders in your life would rationalize, "Well, it might be for the better." They tell you to be optimistic and focus on what you might gain rather than on what you stand to lose. After all, this might be the hand up you've been waiting for. Maybe it leads to a better office, better coworkers, better pay. Perhaps the new role will be more fun, engaging, and meaningful. These rationalizing bystanders are right, of course. You should focus on what you will gain more than on what you'll lose. Optimists are happier in life for a reason.

Still, you and I both know that it's nearly impossible to be balanced in receiving news of an unexpected change. We fear leaving what we will lose, and we hope for some gain. So there must be a third option for better handling the changes that life thrusts upon us, right? We'll get to that shortly, because there's more pain coming your way.

The second reason you likely fear change stems from your *expectation of process pain*. You hear about the new position and department, and you begin to worry about what a colossal undertaking it will be to pack up your office, sort through all those binders, say good-bye to your coworkers, and learn the new skills and lingo of the other department. If the new department is in a different building, you'll have to learn a new route to work, new places for lunch, new parking spots. The entire effort that you'll have to put out is just so overwhelming and frustrating, you feel that going through the process of change is just going to be a colossal pain in the butt.

Naturally, no one is motivated by a pain in the butt, so here, too, you must alter your focus. Rather than zooming in on all the effort that the change will require, bring to the forefront of your mind all the new experiences and relationships that will unfold before you. The mind likes new experiences and relationships but dislikes a pain in the butt. Here, then, your rational friends would say, "Just think, you'll get to meet a ton of new people and learn something new that might challenge you more than what you're doing now." Following this helpful line of advice, you might consider that you'll get to start with a clean slate in this new department and reinvent your personality at work, you'll get to be more assertive than before, you'll be smarter about playing the game, you'll develop more fun and friendship-centered relationships with those around you, and you'll ask more questions and set better expectations at the outset, so that this time, damn it, you own your role and love your people.

Alas, this optimism can be hard to maintain, thanks to the third type of pain you may associate with change: the expectation of *outcome pain*. You think, *Well, sure there are some things to gain here, and yes, the process might be something I can enjoy and really capitalize on, but what if, on the other side of this change, things don't work out, and actually get worse?* Expecting outcome pain means you worry that things won't be good once the change sets in—that the grass won't be greener over there. What if I'm getting phased out? What if I hate my new coworkers? What if I'm not as good at that as I am at this? What if my new boss hates me? What if they do layoffs over there next year? What if their copier isn't as nice as ours?

This expectation is icing on the pudding of pessimism. You add worries about outcome pain to those about loss pain and process pain, and you have completed the triangle of fear. And voilà! There is no chance you will look forward to this change. If the triangle of fear travels to other areas of your life enough times with enough intensity, one day you wake up truly fearful of change.

Hopefully, your rational friends can help stem these fears once more. They'll probably suggest that you stop fixating on the possible long-term negative outcomes and start focusing on the positive ones. They'll say, "You have to make yourself think of the possibilities, not the pitfalls."

Again, this is great advice, which you should heed. Doing so simply involves changing the negative what-if statements you're playing in your mind (What if this doesn't turn out well?) to more positive what-if statements (What if this takes me one step closer?). By focusing on positive outcomes, you might think about how you'll be smarter, happier, and even more secure now that you're in the new role. You might think about the new skills you'll develop, how you'll be more well-rounded and better connected between departments, more valuable, and how all these new possibilities will lead to new results and doors opening for you.

If you think this all sounds like simply pouring optimism over an unwelcome change, you're right. But what's the alternative? You can either welcome change or hate it. You can either consciously direct yourself into feeling positive in life or let yourself be swept into unexamined fear. As always, it's a choice.

It's also important to note that the expectation of these three kinds of pain—loss, process, and outcome—doesn't just arise in us when outside forces introduce a new change into our lives. They also well up when we choose to make a change in our lives. Let's say you finally decide to improve your health, and instead of your boss changing your career, you decide to do it.

You feel motivated, and you think, *It's time to go on a diet, stop smoking, exercise regularly, and get a new job.* Regardless of how pumped you are about making these changes, somewhere in your mind the pains of loss, process, and outcome will rear their ugly heads. You must be prepared to counter them.

To hold down these fears and gain momentum against process pain, you have to stop focusing on the painful effort required to change, and start focusing on the pleasurable experiences that will come from the process. Instead of worrying about the daunting effort required to prepare different meals, you should concentrate on the new experiences you will have: learning new ways to increase your energy and boost your stamina through food, learning to cook tastier meals faster and cheaper, learning to eat foods that are good for you and for the planet, sharing recipes with friends and family, wowing visitors with your fancy, healthy hors d'oeuvres. Take the same approach in reframing your initial concerns about quitting smoking, exercising, or finding a new job. Think, *I'll get to learn newer ways to manage my stress and addictions and, in the process, never again have to be controlled by anything that harms me. I'll have a blast with a new group of people who, like me, are committed to exercise and having more energy. I'll get to brush up on my interview skills and recast myself in the marketplace so I can finally shape what I do, and get paid what I'm worth.* The mantra becomes: change brings new experiences, new lessons, new strengths.

You'll also have to watch out for expectations of outcome pain sneaking up on you. It will be all too tempting to obsess over such questions as *What if I put myself through all this diet hell and don't get any thinner? What if I quit smoking only to start again later on? What if I start exercising and the pounds don't come off? What if I quit my job, and the job I end up with is even worse than the one I left?* The pattern here is that every time you focus on change, you ask yourself a what-if question that ends in a negative statement. What if I fail? What if life gets worse? What if I sacrifice and still don't get what I want?

Again, these types of questions just kill your motivation to make the needed changes to improve your life. Knowing this, you make the switch to positive what-if statements: *What if I put myself through this diet and I do become thinner, healthier, and happier? What if I quit smoking and have the lung capacity to play with the kids and get up the stairs without breathing hard and have the mental and physical control that will allow me never to pick up a cancer stick again? What if I exercise and get leaner and stronger and more defined and I get to buy clothes that show how sexy I can really be? What if I quit my job*

and end up in a career that I absolutely love and that finally lets me
create and contribute at the levels I know I can?

Changing the way you think of change in these ways may be the most powerful mind-set shift you will ever make in your life. But we can't just stop at learning how to turn negatives into positives. At some point, to master your own fate, you actually have to start seeing change as pleasurable in itself, as something that brings in new learning and growth no matter whether it's self-initiated or not. It's at this level, when you enjoy change, that the charge in life really intensifies.

Activator #2: Get Clarity, Think Big, and Be Bold

Of course, fear and the lack of openness to change aren't the only things that prevent people from transforming their lives. Sometimes it's more of a tactical problem than an emotional or conceptual one. For many people, the drive for change stalls simply because they lack clarity and ambition.

Almost all the people I work with at a high level believe they have clarity. They know what they want, or so they tell me. This applies to high performers I've just met as well as the elite movers and shakers I coach on an individual basis. You'd certainly hope the latter would know what they want before they hire me—because I serve primarily through my seminars, I won't coach anyone individually for less than a quarter million dollars a year—but you would be surprised. I've found that very few people, perhaps two in a hundred, actually have real clarity on what they are trying to accomplish in life (let alone what they need to change to get there). It's understandable that not all of us know our lives' purposes. But for everyday changes in our lives, you would imagine that we all know what we're trying to accomplish. Unfortunately, that's just not the case.

The first step in making any change in life is to have a defined, detailed vision for what you want to accomplish. Sounds pretty basic, right? But I'm guessing you would bumble and stutter if I asked you to describe exactly what you *have been* trying to change and achieve in, say, your financial life over the past twelve months. Notice the emphasis here. I'm not asking you what you *want* to change or achieve; I'm asking what you *have been* trying to do. Most people can come up with an answer on the fly to: "What would you like to change and achieve in your financial life in the next year?" But very few can actually tell you what they *have been* trying to achieve, which is an obvious nod to the fact that they haven't been acting on a clear vision. (The cat's out of the bag; now you know how I'd find out if you are really clear about *any* area of your life.)

So how do we get to clarity and choose what we want to do or change? The answer, as is often the case, lies in the question itself. To get clarity, we must choose what to do, which presupposes that we have a buffet of choices in front of us to select from. To find clarity, you have to have choices, and it's this fact alone that stumps so many well-meaning people from ever having clarity in their lives. They forget that they must gather and explore options and opportunities before selecting what to do. This line of questioning explains why so many college graduates don't know what to do with their lives— many don't yet have enough experience in life to be able to choose their careers, passions, or purposes.

Here's my short course on finding clarity: think of an area of your life, and before you decide what to do or change, go do some research to see the universe of options and possibilities available to you in that area. Let's say you're trying to find clarity on your goals in your financial life. It's safe to bet that if you have limited information on your financial options, you'll be less than clear on what you want to do. Something inside you will wonder, *What if I'm missing something here? How can I be sure that I have all the information to make a good choice? I'm not even sure what I want, because I'm not sure what my options are.* It's hard to have vision if you've never seen anything, so begin your efforts to find clarity by gathering research and getting perspective on what your options are. From there, choose what's right for you, model others who've succeeded in your area of interest, and march on.

The most important aspect of clarity is choosing a change that you deeply desire and will be inspired to work toward no matter the challenges that will inevitably lie ahead. More often than not, failing at change happens simply because someone didn't want the change badly enough. So he didn't try hard enough for long enough. It's one of life's great truths: people fight a tough fight only for something they deeply believe in.

The challenge is that we have an epidemic of half-interested wimps running the world. We've let ourselves be neutered of any real desire or grand ambitions for change by heeding the advice of the "realists" and the standard bearers of the status quo, who tell us to set SMART goals (specific, measurable, attainable, relevant, and time-bound). But these types of attainable goals never spark the imagination or fire the will. We are now a culture flooded with goals and spreadsheets and work plans that inspire no heart, no drive, no courage.

The drive for real change—the kind of change that alters the course of your life, business, and greater world—comes from a deep, powerful hunger and desire to do something big and meaningful. No one joins the major leagues to bunt, and no one joins a company so he can (hopefully) one day share an idea with a (hopefully) interested conference room full of bored coworkers. Those living a Charged Life see the crowds on their feet, chanting, calling for greatness, and they want to swing big, go for the fences, and sprint around the bases with a reckless abandon that the "realists" would call madness. Those living a Charged Life can't even see themselves in a conference room of drones. Instead, they see their ideas in the lives of consumers the world over. Real desire is like that: wanting nothing less than the home run and the global contribution. It's that level of drive that incites us to take chances, to give our best efforts and go for broke, not out of foolhardiness but out of blatant disregard for the naysayers and a grand desire to do something that counts.

You want to change? Then do not, under any circumstances, allow yourself to settle on a vision or a calling or a simple change in any arena that is uninspiring. If you're going to have clarity on something in your life, make it something so big and bright and shiny that you will get out of bed and chase it until you grasp it or die. Bring forth a desire that knows no safe boundaries and even scares you a little bit, that will demand all the best that is in you, that takes you out of your own orbit and onto new and unfamiliar ground. That kind of desire changes your life, and it changes the world.

But don't take it from me. Here's a man who had the drive for change and led the United States of America to swing bigger than it had ever imagined—and, in doing so, broke the boundaries of all that we ever knew:

We choose to go to the moon. We choose to go to the moon in this decade and do the other things, not because they are easy, but because they are hard, because that goal will serve to organize and measure the best of our energies and skills, because that challenge is one that we are willing to accept, one we are unwilling to postpone, and one which we intend to win, and the others, too.

To be sure, all this costs us all a good deal of money. . . . Space expenditures will soon rise some more . . . for we have given this program a high national priority—even though I realize that this is in some measure an act of faith and vision, for we do not now know what benefits await us.

But if I were to say, my fellow citizens, that we shall send to the moon, 240,000 miles away from the control station in Houston, a giant rocket more than 300 feet tall, the length of this football field, made of new metal alloys, some of which have not yet been invented, capable of standing heat and stresses several times more than have ever been experienced, fitted together with a precision better than the finest watch, carrying all the equipment needed for propulsion, guidance, control, communications, food and survival, on an untried mission, to an unknown celestial body, and then return it safely to earth, reentering the atmosphere at speeds of over 25,000 miles per hour, causing heat about half that of the temperature of the sun—almost as hot as it is here today—and do all this, and do it right, and do it first before this decade is out—then we must be bold.

Many years ago the great British explorer George Mallory, who was to die on Mount Everest, was asked why did he want to climb it. He said, "Because it is there."

Well, space is there, and we're going to climb it, and the moon and the planets are there, and new hopes for knowledge and peace are there. And, therefore, as we set sail we ask God's blessing on the most hazardous and dangerous and greatest adventure on which man has ever embarked.

—PRESIDENT JOHN F. KENNEDY, SEPTEMBER 12, 1962

You want to change your life? Be bold once again. Find your moon. Chase something so big and exciting it's unimaginable to you and those around you. Be brave enough to take action, test things out, fail, get up again, fail again, get embarrassed for trying, fail some more, get up again and smile, and keep moving—this is the stuff of courage, and the only approach to change that will fuel your charge and help your life truly lift off.

Activator #3: Make Real Choices

As you boldly move forward to a clearly defined vision, be just as clear about what you want and don't want on your journey. Make real choices *in advance* of setting out on any new endeavor.

This brings me to one of the simple but immensely popular tools we use at High Performance Academy. It's called the "This-That Rule Tool." You can download the tool at www.TheChargeBook.com/resources.

The idea is that you should create statements about things you want (this) and about things you don't want (that), so that you are both clear and focused on your journey to change. This is about you making real choices by having you make these statements:

1. I want this, not that.
2. Do more of this, no more of that.
3. When this happens, do that.
4. Always choose this, not that.
5. Do this now, then that.

1. I want this, not that. Before you plan anything, be razor sharp and diamond clear about what you want *and* what you don't want. It's astounding how many people don't deeply consider what they *don't* want. They rush toward some goal or objective and often hit it, only to be miserable at the end. This is the cliché of the guy who wants a million dollars and works harder than hell to get it and *does*—at the cost of his real passions, his health, and his family. He winds up a millionaire but realizes that money wasn't the only thing he wanted from his life. Imagine if he had said, *"I want to have a million dollars in my bank account in ten years [this], but I don't ever want to get stuck doing administrative stuff I don't love, I don't want to get fat and unhealthy, and I don't ever want to work on weekends or lose connection with my family [that].*" If he'd had the vision to keep this in front of him and follow through on it, I'm guessing his life would have turned out differently. Sometimes it's important to keep one eye on the moon and another on the dial that tells you if you're in trouble.

2. Do more of this, no more of that. To reach any desired goal, we have to start or continue some things, and we have to stop others. Being clear about these start-stop actions is critical to know as you plan your route to victory. Let's continue with our friend who became a millionaire at the expense of his passion, health, and family. Wouldn't he have been better off if he had set a few rules that said: Do more delegating. Do more creative work that engages you. Do more healthy meals. Do more date nights with your wife and more weekend outings with your kids. No more can you allow others to own your agenda and dictate your work and passions. No more can you eat fast food or miss an entire week at the gym. No more can you forget birthdays.

3. When this happens, do that. I've learned the incredible power of asking clients to hook a new behavior onto the back of an existing one—what I call the "habit hook." For example, let's say I have a client who is a mother of three, works from home, and wants to lose some weight. She's tried dieting and exercise, but she can't seem to find rhythm or results. One of my first moves would be to find out what her routines and habits already are, then "hook on" other new habits to those. I might find out that she drops her kids off at school every other day, alternating with her husband. If my plan for her involves exercise, I might suggest that she hook exercise onto her habit of dropping off her kids. Her new rule becomes this: *When I drop my kids off at school [this], then I will immediately go to the gym from there [that].*

Our miserable millionaire could have created rules like these: *When I break for lunch every day, I'll text my wife and flirt with her. When I go into meetings, I'll always share at least one idea I'm passionate about. When I leave work, I'll pick up some fresh vegetables on the way home. When I get home, I'll immediately greet my kids and ask how their day went, and I'll be present and actually hear their answers.*

Hooking new habits onto old habits is beyond powerful, and you should take some time to think about how you can do this when creating your plan for change.

4. Always choose this, not that. Life inevitably intercepts the path we've imagined to reach our goals. Storms blow in; tactics fail; good intentions bring bad outcomes. That's the way of the world. In times of uncertainty, conflict, trial, and failure, what kinds of choices will you make? This rule is meant to help you set some ground rules that you can refer to when those circumstances arise. Consider what would have happened for our miserable millionaire had he made the following rules:

- Always choose my passion [this] over short-term profit [that].
- Always choose a salad [this] rather than fries [that].
- Always choose the games I've committed to attend for my kids [this] over the random work opportunity [that].

Rules like these are a blast to think about and write down, because they automatically call forth our highest standards and character.

5. *Do this now, then that.* Most of the tough choices in life have to do with the now-versus-later dilemma. Without consciousness of this fact, and a good set of rules, we're constantly in turmoil about when to act. I had interviewed dozens of people in my field about how and when they expanded, and after hearing of all the distress and distraction that growing too fast had caused, I set some rules for myself. You should do likewise.

To complete our miserable millionaire's story, imagine if he had started with his own set of rules that said this: *I'll run the company for the next five years [this now]. Then I'll delegate more and have someone else running it by the seventh year, when my kids turn ten [then that]. I will start cardio exercise once a week this week [this now]. Then, after the fourth week, I'll add strength training [then that]. Take two weeks vacation with my family this year [this now], and then next year add another two weeks [then that].*

These are simple and short examples. Your own rules shouldn't be—take your time to think through your rules, and write out pages and pages of them. Then keep your "rule book" by your side at all times, revisiting and rewriting it at least once a month for the rest of your life. If that sounds like too much work, no problem; I'm sure you'll do fine following the same system you've been following all these years, and you'll be pleased to get exactly the same results next year as you've gotten this year. I'm teasing, of course. Same system, same results. New system, new results. Try mine and let me know how it turns out for you.

CHARGE POINTS

1. A major change I've been holding back from making in my life because of an expectation of loss, process, or outcome pain is . . .

2. A clear and bold new change I could make in my life would be to . . .

3. The this-that rules I can apply to this clear and bold new change would be . . .

Chapter Nine

THE DRIVE FOR
CHALLENGE

Cowards die many times before their deaths;
the valiant never taste of death but once.
—William Shakespeare, *Julius Caesar*

It's just not worth the risk."

I'm having a conversation with a megastar who built her music and television career on pushing the envelope. After spending an hour passionately describing a new show she wants to produce, she says it would "change television as we know it." I like her immediately because she accidentally swears when she gets excited. It's not that I like swearing per se; it's that I like to see people losing themselves in their enthusiasm.

"The risk?" I ask.

"Yeah. In Hollywood you're only as good as your last show. If I take the risk and the show doesn't hit, then I'm finished."

"Is that true?" I ask. "It seems a lot of stars and directors bomb with movies and shows. If that weren't the case, we'd never have this constant conversation about so-and-so's big comeback."

"Yeah, well, that's what everyone thinks," she says, and sips from her lemonade. "But for every comeback, there are a thousand of us stuck in purgatory. Don't believe everything you hear."

I feel the charge stir in my gut, and I want to do my thing, tell this woman that life can be so much more engaging and full and alive if she'd risk for her passions. But she is famous beyond belief, and I'm not here as a coach but as a guest.

I hold back, and she casually jumps to another subject with our mutual friend who introduced us. The two of them are carrying on for a few minutes. I try to be present but find myself staring at her pool and beautifully landscaped backyard, lost in thought about what she said. Finally, I can't hold back.

"I'm sorry to interrupt," I say. "Something's bothering me, and if I don't say it, I'll hate myself and I wouldn't be a good friend." I look at her directly. "I'd rather burn than compromise my artistry and passions just to walk on eggshells. You must feel the same. I say screw it—follow your passion; do your show."

Both she and my friend laugh at my intensity. Hers is more of a you're-such-a-cute-young-naive-boy laugh. My friend's is a laugh of surprise tinged with embarrassment.

I hold the line. "Tell me why I'm wrong. I mean, you just exploded with enthusiasm about this idea for an entire hour. Why not go for it? What do you have to prove anymore?" She doesn't know I'm setting her up.

"Well, it's not about proving something. I've got my star on the Walk. It's just, you have to be smart with your career these days. Maybe someday I'll do my own thing, but for now I'll just keep the project on the back burner for a while."

I know I'm too aggressive with other people. I push my charge agenda on them too often, and with too much egging on and intensity. I really want to have a good lunch with this woman and my friend today and not screw it up. She has millions of fans, and I love her work. I don't want to be out of line, but I have to live congruently. I must be the bold person I believe myself to be.

"The *someday* syndrome? You're screwed."

She and my friend both look at me in surprise. I get away with it only because of the big, teasing grin on my face.

"You won't do it *someday* any more than someone else will someday reach for her dreams. And I think you're also wrong. You *do* have something to prove. I think you have to prove that you're relevant, and you can't do that by playing safe. Icons and legends don't play that way. I also think you have to prove to yourself that you're not a pushover and that you're someone who follows her dream rather than sells it out for some kind of false safety. Life isn't lived in safety; it's lived in the crucible of challenge. The alternative is becoming a forgotten cokehead, and you don't want that." I smile teasingly again, and she and my friend laugh again.

"Okay. You don't have to persuade an artist that she needs to push the boundaries and be relevant to be noticed and feel fulfilled." She says this in such a way that I know I'm on good footing with her. But then she surprises me. "But what if I do this because you tell me to and it bombs? What responsibility do *you* have? It's easy to motivate others when your name and reputation aren't on the line. What if it goes badly? They're not going to trash you on the front pages."

This is a great question, and it makes me like her even more.

"You're right. I don't have any stake in the game, and I can't fathom having your fame and all that goes along with it. I'm just some guy who showed up at your house and is drinking all your lemonade. But tell you what—if you do challenge yourself to do this show and it doesn't work out, I'll feel horrible, because as much as that's your artistry, *this* is *my* artistry: encouraging and challenging others to go for their dreams. So I do have skin in the game. My name is on the line with you, right now. You have a vision and a dream. Don't let it die in the daylight. Fight for it. Don't do it because it's safe or would please others. Do it because it burns in your gut to do. If you're going to play it safe, you might as well retire now and play golf with the rest of the fat-cat old-white-men crowd in Hollywood. Don't do that. Be the icon and *lead* this industry. Choose your artistry and challenge yourself to think as big and bold as it took to get you where you are today. And if you have the guts, go even bigger."

She looks back at me, and the cold stare is now a direct look that you see in someone's eyes only once the gauntlet of challenge has been dropped and the person is picking it up—the you're-goddamn-right-I-will expression that precedes greatness.

She nods her head. "I'll change television with this."

I just nod with her and return the look of certainty.

She keeps nodding, committing to it, putting the plan in place in her brain. Then she looks to our friend. "I see why you brought this guy. I needed someone to poke at me."

• • •

There is but one word to bring to the center of your mind, which can define the path to an engaged life and mobilize the great energies of potential within you: *challenge*.

All the psychological and spiritual growth you've experienced as a human being has been a result of what I call "real challenge." It was the stretching of your self-concept, skills, beliefs, and mental or physical capacities that were brought about by a greater demand from you or your environment. It was in those moments that your concentration was galvanized, your skill and best efforts called upon, and your will, strength, and courage tested. These were the moments when the struggle meant something to you and you focused on the activity at hand in such a way that your sense of time and your self-consciousness just seemed to melt away. These were the sweet-spot moments when you surprised even yourself, rising above your own limits and hitting a higher gear of effort, creativity, and consciousness. That's when real change and growth happened. And I'll wager that's when you felt more alive and engaged—more *charged*—than ever.

These days, we all have plenty of goals on our daily planners and are busy enough multitasking, serving competing interests, trying to please our bosses, partners, and kids. But there's a big difference between being truly challenged and just busily checking off your daily tick list or carrying the cross of others' expectations. These distinctions light the way to your highest happiness.

It's important to differentiate between goals and challenges. A goal can simply be an item on a to-do list or checklist. Nothing in setting a goal demands the most of you; a *challenge*, on the other hand, is something that stretches your efforts and abilities. Goal thinking is destination thinking—it's all about getting something. Challenge thinking immediately inspires thoughts about the journey—it's about giving something more of *yourself*. In this chapter, I'll cover more about destination versus journey, and the five criteria of a good challenge.

You should also be aware that being busy is not the same as being challenged, just as change is not the same as progress. We spend much of our lives busily completing mundane maintenance activities—getting ourselves up and fed, commuting to and from work, cleaning, shopping, and organizing. Sure we have to-do lists and checklists, and we have to manage it all and still remember to pick up the kids, but if we're honest, these activities are hardly challenging the boundaries of our abilities.

For the most part, the stress people feel in life is rarely related to real challenge, the kind that stretches our abilities and makes us feel engaged and growing. Most stress today comes from distraction and procrastination. In these times of information overload and speedy Internet access, too many of us simply spend too much time on unimportant activities and end up being caught in a time crunch. Add to that our tendency to procrastinate because we don't really care about the activities we're supposed to do, and suddenly the overwhelm really kicks in as more and more deadlines come due.

Of course, there are plenty of external stressors too. We feel like we're always busy, so it's just "not possible to take on any more" in our lives. Or, as our star felt at the beginning of the chapter, we fear the repercussions of taking new risks. The good news is that these are all nonsense excuses, and I promised you at the beginning of this book that I will bring the battle call. In this chapter, I am here to tell you that it's time to rise above the mundane murmur of what "they" want you to do with your life. It's time to hit the gas pedal of your potential hard and finally activate this drive for challenge in a way that brings back the zest of engagement and progress in your life. You can feel more energy in life, and the way to do it is to summon your greatest energies toward real challenges.

Activator #1: Choose Fulfilling Challenges

Challenge is the pathway to engagement and progress in our lives. But not all challenges are created equal. Some challenges make us feel alive, engaged, connected, and fulfilled. Others simply overwhelm us. Knowing the difference as you set bigger and bolder challenges for yourself is critical to your sanity, success, and satisfaction.

How do you choose "good" challenges? It helps to know that the kind of challenges that bring full engagement and fulfillment in our lives have five things in common. First, they demand *singularity of focus*, meaning they are mighty enough activities that they require our full and undivided attention and concentration in the moment. These challenges, then, are not insignificant, nor do they allow multitasking. They absorb us because they engage both our mental and our physical presence. Painting a picture, teaching your kids an activity, designing a website, creating or giving a presentation—all are examples of efforts that require you to focus. To inspire a singularity of focus, a challenge must be important to you and it must be something you feel you should do now in this moment. If it's trivial or not time-bound, you won't engage. So in selecting your next challenge in life, choose one that is meaningful and will demand your complete concentration.

Second, great challenges *stretch our efforts and capabilities*, demanding slightly more than the best of our skills and strengths. They are just over and above our current abilities, so they require us to engage fully . . . and grow. The secret here is to select challenges that extend just beyond your comfort zones. Knowing this secret explains why so many of us have become fascinated with video games. Have you ever played a video game that *didn't* have escalating levels of difficulty? Well, life can feel like play, too, when we purposefully engage in activities that demand we test and develop our skills. If you're a good public speaker who always uses notes, choosing to go without notes in your next presentation will stretch you. If you're a good racquetball player, playing a competitor who is better than you will demand more of you. If you're an executive, take on a project that's slightly over your head. You needn't decide to skip from level one of difficulty to level ten; that just causes you to feel overwhelmed. Instead, approach your next challenge as an opportunity to go from level one to level two or three, and you'll meet the criteria for a satisfying challenge.

Third is the ability to *score performance*. This means that you have the opportunity to know how you're doing—either to self-assess your progress or to get outside feedback. Running often becomes a more satisfying experience when we can measure how fast and far we've gone. Presentations and vocal performances are more fulfilling if we can see the audience's faces and reactions to our voice. Dieting is more engaging when we can stand on the scales and see how we're doing. While all this sounds intuitive, the surprising fact is that few people purposely build progress checks into their challenges. They simply get inspired, start out, and then give up when they no longer "feel like" continuing. But a hit of motivation, either in seeing results or in getting redirected, often happens at the checkpoints in any endeavor. So craft your next challenge with the intention of assessing your progress along the way.

Fourth, satisfying challenges allow for a *sense of completion*. People can run a marathon because they know that their challenge has a finish line. Executives who work around the clock, fully engaged in a project, do so because they have a deadline to hit that they believe matters to their overall challenge of contributing fully and rising to the top. These examples illustrate that having a few finish lines in mind and the belief in a payoff are incredibly important in enduring the stretch of any challenge. This concept becomes even more important as we take on bigger and bigger challenges. For example, if you're going to take on the challenge of ending world poverty, you have to construct the challenge and your expectations in such a way that you feel you are completing significant milestones. If you just toil away all day for forty years at the challenge but never feel a gratifying sense of completing important and meaningful projects, you will lose your sense of engagement. This is why organizational-change agents will always design *small wins* into a change plan. Such wins give an opportunity to score performance—*we're succeeding!*—but also provide moments when people sense they have completed something important—*we finished that!*

Finally, challenges that enliven you are those that allow a *sharing of experience and achievement*. Climbing Mount Everest would hit all our previous criteria, and that alone would make it a wonderfully satisfying experience. But climbing Everest *with someone else* would feel infinitely better. Standing atop a mountain and jumping in place to celebrate feels terrific; getting to do so and then turning to hug someone and recognize the experience and achievement together is indescribably more fulfilling. Not all sharing need be so epic. Attempting to stitch a more complex quilt fits the first four criteria as well. What makes the activity ultimately satisfying, though, is showing the new quilt to your loved ones, who can ooh and aah and celebrate or, ultimately, enjoy your creation. Often, it's *talking about and celebrating* how we have faced and triumphed over our challenges that put the icing on the cake. It's important that you understand how vital this is to your psyche and desire to take on more and more complex challenges. Even if you overcome a tremendous challenge and feel the personal victory, it's simply not powerful enough. It may activate your left brain, which says, *I have achieved*, but it will not activate your more social right brain, which desperately desires to say, *Look, Ma, I did it!*

Imagine the difference in feeling in the following scenarios. You train hard to complete a marathon, and after pushing your mind and body beyond what you knew was possible over 26.2 miles, you finally cross the finish line and raise your arms in victory. In one ending to the story, you now simply walk alone over to your car, go home, take a shower, and never speak of it again. In the other, you hug your fellow runners and those who have come to lend support, and you go to lunch with a few close friends and family members and talk about the slog, the fight, the magic of crossing a threshold of possibility. You decide: Which *feels* more meaningful and fulfilling?

These are the criteria to creating and experiencing challenges that truly make you feel alive:

- Singularity of focus
- Stretch of effort and capability
- Scoring of performance
- Sense of completion
- Sharing of experience and result

I imagine, if you reflect on any joyous moment of triumph or engagement in your life, these factors were at play. Now that you are conscious of them, use them to intelligently and strategically craft new challenges for yourself.

Activator #2: Focus on the Journey and Don't Fear Rejection

As you're leaping mountains and conquering the world, it's good to know in advance where you'll get stuck. Inevitably, we all face new doubts and fears as we take on greater and greater challenges, so I would be remiss not to address them here.

There tend to be two mental villains we all face when fighting the good fight on the path to a new dream: unmet expectations and a paralizing fear of rejection.

We all can relate to unmet expectations. We've all engaged and worked our tails off on projects in the past only to feel that we weren't rewarded or recognized as much as we had hoped or deserved. That's life. And because that's life, it's time we changed our entire approach to what we expect from challenge. To live a Charged Life, you've got to alter your beliefs about *why* to take on a challenge.

For most people, taking on a challenge is all about the outcome—the reward at the end of the road of effort. They accept new projects at work because they believe they will get them raises. They decide to lose weight because it will make them fit into smaller jeans. They learn a language so they can order food in another country. They take on a competitor to win a trophy and the crowd's admiration. In each case, these people are chasing results.

Focusing on the destination rather than the journey is something we're culturally conditioned to do at the earliest stages of life. The challenge of learning the alphabet is to get the gold star. Studying and working hard gets us a good report card . . . and acceptance into a good college . . . and then a good job . . . and a better paycheck . . . and the ability to afford the nice house and nice car . . . and then the better house and more cars . . . and on and on it goes. This study-hard, work-hard dynamic, we're told, will lead us to everything we ever wanted (usually something we were told we should want): money, wealth, power, status, achievement, accumulation.

All these rewards of effort are extrinsic rewards, received from the outside world. Unfortunately, our lives become about taking on challenges that are driven by such rewards, and, suddenly, we wake up one day and feel dead inside.

Why? Because extrinsic rewards, as I've shared before, don't actually satisfy us. Money moves the happiness needle up only until you get around the average income of the country you live in. Fame, power, status, and materialistic accumulation usually move the needle up only a few points, just in the first year or so that you have them, and mostly only because the feeling of having these trappings is novel and may inspire pride (and then only if you really earned it through your direct efforts). The catch with extrinsic rewards is that they're never enough and they set us on a slowly increasing incline on the treadmill of *more*. One day we wake up with many of the extrinsic rewards we've been chasing for so long, yet we feel nothing about them.

To avoid this, we've got to follow the wisdom of the ancients, who told us to *focus on the journey rather than the destination*. Don't worry whether you'll succeed at the highest level or not as you're on the journey. Instead, be in the moment during the journey: Enjoy it, live it, and learn from it. Pay attention to what's in front of you one step at a time, relishing in your efforts and the new knowledge, skills, and abilities you're picking up along the way. Learn to enjoy the process of taking on your challenges and *celebrating your own effort* as much as your results. The more you focus on the journey, the more challenges feel engaging and surmountable.

Of course, this is all great personal-development advice, but realists will say that people are too scared to take on big challenges and free themselves from the outcomes because human beings, they say, are so scared of failure and social rejection. If you're like a lot of my readers, one reason you don't take on bigger challenges in life is because you're afraid of how others will judge you as you embark (or fail). So let's take this fear of rejection head-on so you can overcome it.

It turns out social rejection isn't something that happens as often as you fear. I've asked audiences from around the globe this question: "How many times have you been rejected in a way that really, deeply hurt you? I'm not talking about one of those small embarrassing moments when someone said they didn't like your shoes or your hair. I mean the kind of rejection that really hurt, that stopped you from being you or forever altered your identity. I mean a rejection that really hurt and really mattered. How many times?"

I've asked this question of my audiences from all over the world. The average age of my audience is forty to fifty-five, so they're not green around the ears. Sixty percent are women, most with families, most making a higher-than-normal income in the countries where they reside. I'll usually ask people to raise their hands as I increase the number: "How many times? Twice? Five times? Seven? Ten? Fifteen? Twenty?"

Among hundreds of audiences and hundreds of thousands of people, the average of the responses has never changed: seven. Most people, in the course of their lives leading up to retirement, have been rejected in a way that really hurt just seven times.

I usually follow up this question by asking the audiences to count the opposite. "How many times have you been encouraged by another person in your life in such a way that it had a very *positive* effect on your life?" I ask the same type of follow-up question: "How many of you have been accepted, cheered on, and encouraged in this way once? Twice? Five times? Seven? Ten? Fifteen? Twenty?" When I do this, the audience breaks into rolling laughter. Everyone in the room still has his or her hand up at twenty. So I keep going. "How many would guess it's been a hundred times? Five hundred? A thousand? More than a thousand?" Every hand up in the room is still up.

Here's what's fascinating about all this. We all fear rejection, yet *it turns out that significant rejection barely ever happens*. Most adults can recall having been rejected in a way that had real impact on their lives or identities only seven times.

So the thing holding us back from taking on bigger challenges in life barely ever happens. Even if it happened a hundred times by the time we were forty years old, would that still be enough to convince you to quit taking risks, expressing yourself, going for it? Not me.

But don't miss the rest of the story. While seven may be the average number of people who have significantly rejected us by the time we hit adulthood, the counter to that is the *thousands* of times we've been supported or encouraged. We went to school with hundreds if not thousands of people, worked with or interacted with hundreds if not thousands of people in our adult lives (coworkers, customers, neighbors, Facebook strangers), and in general, they were accepting or supportive. If they were not supportive, perhaps they just let us do our own thing, but at least they didn't judge or reject us in a way that altered our identities.

All this leads me to ask one question: On the road to your destiny, who and what are you going to pay attention to? The seven or eight mean people—whose judgments were much more about themselves than you—who are in your rearview mirror? Or the thousands of cheers and encouragements you've received that are now lining your path to progress? You choose.

Overlaying seven people's actions, no matter how hurtful, onto your expectations for the rest of humanity is neither fair nor healthy. There are, of course, people in the world who simply take pleasure in judging others and letting everyone know about it. These are the haters, cynics, and critics. These are people whom the megastar from the beginning of the chapter feared but ultimately overcame (and she was nominated for an Emmy).

Rather than give these critics power over you or your future, simply ignore them or, at your most generous, have sympathy for them. These are the weak who can sense a surge of power only by preying on the perceived weaknesses of others. These are the ones who have lost their dreams and their connection to hope and humanity. It is these people whom you must never let grab hold of your ambitions and strangle your drive for challenging yourself, others, or society. Their hateful and uninformed opinions are insignificant, and you mustn't let your dreams die just because someone takes aim at you as you march to the mountaintop.

I'll conclude with my favorite quote on the subject:

It is not the critic who counts; not the man who points out how the strong man stumbles, or where the doer of deeds could have done them better. The credit belongs to the man who is actually in the arena, whose face is marred by dust and sweat and blood; who strives valiantly; who errs, who comes short again and again, because there is no effort without error and shortcoming; but who does actually strive to do the deeds; who knows great enthusiasms, the great devotions; who spends himself in a worthy cause; who at the best knows in the end the triumph of high achievement, and who at the worst, if he fails, at least fails while daring greatly, so that his place shall never be with those cold and timid souls who know neither victory nor defeat.

—THEODORE ROOSEVELT, EXCERPT FROM THE SPEECH
"CITIZENSHIP IN A REPUBLIC," DELIVERED AT THE
SORBONNE, PARIS, APRIL 23, 1910

Activator #3: Set Monthly Thirty-Day Challenges

I've set one personal challenge for myself every single month for fifteen years. As a creative, "right-brained" person, this took *tremendous discipline* for me. But both the journeys and the destinations (so far, anyway) have been more engaging and satisfying than I could ever have fathomed. I've felt truly *alive* every single month of my life (in fact, almost every day) since I made the decision to do so. My days are lit with authentic flow and fulfillment because I'm always engaged in passionate pursuits and challenges. In the past amazingly fun and exciting decade and a half, I've felt all the intrinsic and extrinsic rewards that go with a life fully lived. I do work that I love and find meaningful, I've built several million-dollar brands, and I've secured my family's future to the best of my abilities. Believe me, I've fallen on my face thousands of times, but always with a joyful attitude, knowing that, if nothing else, I was learning—failing forward. I've met presidents of countries, traveled the globe, purchased homes for family members, given millions of dollars to causes and pursuits I deeply believe in. My friend Paulo Coelho says that one of the greatest things about America is that we can share our successes with pride, as illustrations of what is possible, without being judged vain. I hope that's true and that you can see that I don't share any of this to impress anyone but, rather, to illustrate the potential of setting consistent challenges for yourself.

I attribute almost all my personal and financial successes to God first, to my family and mentors second, and, third, to the ways I've challenged myself and chosen to meet life's challenges. Of the latter, the best thing I've ever done is set monthly challenges for myself.

A monthly personal challenge might be to try a new sport, learn a new skill, take on a big creative project, perform at higher levels in a series of meetings, or simply embrace a new belief. My recent months' challenges have been to improve my listening skills, become a better racquetball player, and create more training videos for my fans.

I always highlight one challenge every single month and approach it with zeal and discipline. Like any skill, setting and working hard to meet personal challenges takes focus, discipline, and commitment. Luckily, the more you do it, the more you enjoy it, and the more the drive for challenge becomes activated and part of your life again.

To begin, take out a piece of paper right now. Draw twelve boxes on the page, each representing one month of the year. Inside each box, write a one-to-four-word description of a challenge you're going to take on during that month. Maybe you'll write "listen," "train harder for marathon," "design website," "master my diet," or simply "love."

Whatever your challenge, realize that it's often not the name or topic of the challenge that makes all this so important. It's simply setting real challenges that mean something to you, that stretch you, that make you a better, stronger human being. You can become the master of your own fate by setting up real challenges and knocking them down, enjoying and sharing the process all along the way.

A few thoughts on the types of challenges you set. So far, we've covered personal-development challenges. There are also social and giving challenges you might want to set.

I force myself to set a social challenge once a month to go along with my personal challenge, again on the first of a month, with a check-in every Sunday and another at the end of the month. Social challenges are goals that require you to improve your interactions with other human beings. These are efforts to better your listening, empathy, forgiveness, acceptance, camaraderie, leadership, team-work, sharing, networking, and loving skills, to name a few. They are also efforts to *get out more* and interact with new groups and networks of people.

On the same piece of paper you've used for setting personal challenges, set your social challenges.

Finally, be sure to set a few *giving* challenges for yourself throughout the year related to a cause that you believe needs some smarts, volunteer power, or money. Others would use the phrase "social issues" here, but I don't want to confuse this with the previous challenge, nor do I believe issues are social. To me, the great challenges we face in our time—poverty, war, lack of education, struggling economy, environmental degradation, hunger, inadequate housing and health care—are all world issues. They affect everyone in every society, and if we don't get a handle on them, the world itself, not just society, is in peril.

With this in mind, focus a few of your months' challenges on contributing to the world—a do-gooder challenge that really engages you and propels you to make a difference.

Keeping with the theme of this chapter, a final word about creating social and giving challenges for yourself: don't attempt to make a difference in a halfhearted way—*push yourself* to do great things for great causes. I know, it's easy to become resigned in today's troubled world, thinking you can't do anything significant to help change it. Today's issues are daunting. Too many people living below the poverty line. Millions lacking access to clean water, food, sanitation, medical care, opportunity. Trillions of dollars in national debt. Markets collapsing. Wars raging. Politicians in gridlock. The environment going to hell.

These challenges are serious and make up some of the defining issues of our times. While one would hope that all the news coverage on these issues would spread education and commitment for dealing with them, the opposite has proved true. Today's news rarely educates or inspires anything but contempt and polarization. In a quest for ratings, even the best news coverage has become salacious—

Alert! Alert! Alert!—and merely reports on the extreme perspectives on any issue. This leads to no real information, only positions, and no real dialogues that spur discovery or solutions. Worse, in their efforts to incite controversy, the media have enlisted us all in a societal soup of endless, thoughtless, and fruitless blame games.

As we watch all this from our armchairs of abundance, we simply tune out. Resignation sets in—not to get involved but simply to get incensed. We follow the news anchors' tones of "*Tsk tsk*, how dare they!" But we remain largely apathetic. We hate what we see happening, but the issues are so large, we simply think, *Oh well, what could I possibly do?*

What you can do is beyond your current imagination. And yet that's the problem. Because it lies "beyond" your present imagination, it's difficult to grasp except by the visionary few who dare see themselves boldly venturing into the territory of the impossible. So the visionaries feel they can change the world, while the rest of society digs itself into ruts of resignation.

But we all can be greater visionaries and contributors by adopting two simple perspectives. First, we must stop thinking that it's worthwhile to address a challenge only if it's solvable. You alone will not solve world poverty. You will not fix education, the economy, or the environment. But you can choose to be part of the solution. And it's being part of a solution and taking on a challenge that makes us feel alive, even if we never get to see the fruits of our labors in our lifetimes. Jump into a challenge, and you'll start feeling like part of the solution.

Second, to loosen the reins of resignation, we must stop thinking we have to address these problems alone. Doing our part is important, but we must focus as much on being part of, or creating, a community of committed people to address our world's most pressing needs.

Margaret Mead said it best: "Never underestimate the power of a few committed people to change the world. Indeed, it is the only thing that ever has."

It's time to reengage with society's problems and challenges. Doing so will likely never lead to extrinsic rewards or total solutions that you'll see in your lifetime. But it's not about the destination; it's about the journey and feeling as though we did something with our lives that helped the world.

If you want to feel better about life, you have to feel better about the world. The best way to do that is to challenge yourself to be an active participant in society. Being part of the solution always feels better than being a spectator. If you simply watch a sinking ship and do nothing, you will feel dead inside. But jump in the rescue boats, mobilize those around you to do the same, and, suddenly, you'll feel alive again.

CHARGE POINTS

1. The next big and bold challenge I'm going to take on in my life is to . . .

2. If I stopped fearing rejection, a challenge I would have taken on earlier in my life would have been to . . .

3. The thirty-day challenges I could set for myself over the next twelve months include . . .

Chapter Ten

THE DRIVE FOR
CREATIVE EXPRESSION

*There is a vitality, a life force, an energy, a quickening, that is
translated through you into action, and because there is only
one you in all time, this expression is unique. And, if you block
it, it will never exist through any other medium and will be lost.*
—Martha Graham

Y ou need to lose the red hair if anyone is going to take you
seriously."

The woman sitting next to me on stage, a famous spiritual "guru,"
is talking to a bright-eyed young woman in the front row, named
Sasha, who has a bright red streak running through her thick, long
black hair. The entire audience, including Sasha and me, is surprised.
After preaching self-acceptance and personal power for nearly an
hour, the guru is giving unsolicited advice to Sasha that the red
streak in her hair will prevent her from being accepted by others,
especially members of the buttoned-up media.

The guru seems to miss the audience's shock, going on to share a
few more pieces of advice with Sasha before changing the subject. I
sit in silence, steaming in anger under the bright lights of the stage.

I feel as if the eight hundred people in the audience want me to say something, but I'm not sure what I feel at the moment or why.

When we finish our conversation, the audience seems to have forgotten the incident and gives a strong round of applause. But something still feels amiss.

That night and the next morning, I sort through my feelings and discover the source of my anger. The guru's comments upset me because they were incongruent with what she had been sharing and, more specifically, were a violation of the relationship with my audience member. Sasha hadn't asked the guru a question or sought advice. She was just sitting there, unsuspecting, when the guru went at her in an attempt to share why we all must keep a professional image.

When I'm angry, boy, do I clap. That morning I bounded onto the stage as I usually do, revving the entire audience up to clap with me. This time, I went extra long with the clapping and dancing, and the room felt set to explode.

I started right at it. "One of the things I love most about the expert industry—what I call the how-to advice space—is how many different voices and perspectives there are. I learn from everyone, and I know you all do, too. But we each have our unique ways of interpreting things, and we each have our unique approaches to giving advice."

I look down at the front row, looking for Sasha. When I spot her, I say directly to her, "For example, had I seen the woman in the front row with the red hair last night, I would have said, 'Go on with your bad self, girl!'"

The second I finish the sentence, the audience roars with approval. It's obvious the guru's admonishment and advice to Sasha the night before had affected her deeply—today her hair is pulled back tight in a ponytail, and she's wearing a suit. She looks like a different person: more severe, contained. But the facade cracks quickly when I say this from the stage, and she bursts into tears faster than I've ever seen a woman cry.

My camera guys zoom in on Sasha, and the crowd starts screaming and clapping for her. I say, "Sasha, please come up to the stage," and the audience jumps to its feet, roaring with excitement and support for her. The level of energy in the room goes to ten.

I grab a microphone and hand it to Sasha, who at this point is crying at the mascara-all-over-the-face level. I ask, "So, what's up with the red hair?"

She laughs and tries to center herself, then replies, "It's just my way of reminding myself to be wild and creative and hot, to be fully myself, every time I look in the mirror. It reminds me to let the strand of my own sensuality shine through."

Another round of riotous applause from the audience.

Then I ask, "So, Sasha, what do you do?"

At this point, she stands taller and, with full presence, says, "I teach women to tap into that part of themselves that is wild and free and fully expressed. I teach them not to hide behind false facades but to feel beautiful in their own skin and live who they are: sensual, gorgeous, creative, free-spirited beings who deserve love and live through love."

The audience leaps to its feet and gives a standing ovation unlike anything I've ever witnessed. Sasha turns out to be one of the most articulate and passionate women I had on my stage that weekend, and the audience feels it. Never in my life, in fact, have I sensed an audience wanting someone to be recognized and accepted as much as they did Sasha. They, too, felt that the guru's comments the night before were not just incongruent but also an affront to the individuality and creative spirit that lives within us all. By honoring Sasha, they are honoring the wild and free within themselves.

I ask the audience to help me cement in Sasha's knowledge that she is beautiful just the way she is, by serenading her. I lead them in singing a few lines from Joe Cocker's song "You Are So Beautiful."

Later that night, I invited Sasha and her brother to our VIP dinner for our best clients. When I meet her brother, who is years younger than she, he pulls me aside and says, "I want to thank you for what you did for my sister today. Last night, when the speaker judged her in such an open way, everything in me as a brother and a man wanted to fight back and protect her. I think the whole audience felt voiceless, but we all wanted to fight for Sasha. The fact that you took the time this morning to acknowledge it and recognize my sister meant the world to her. It literally changed her life. And it made you my brother."

. . .

I believe there is nothing more powerful in life than allowing our own individuality to shine through, to light the world with our own divine uniqueness. For some people, part of that expression means dyeing a swatch of their hair red. For others, it's creatively expressing themselves through their work, art, music, or daily interactions with others. Whatever it is, we know one thing: never attempt to squelch another human being's individuality or creative expression. Fortunately, most of our world and even the economy now celebrates the creative spirit and rewards it in so many ways. When we post a creative video, it gets hits. When we share creative ideas, we get promoted. When we stand before an audience and bare our hearts and celebrate our own magic, they stand and applaud.

The drive for creative expression urges us to physically and socially manifest our unique talents, strengths, and perspectives. More simply, you are who you are, and you are different from others because of the unique way you express yourself.

When you feel in touch with your creative side and express it consistently you feel more alive and engaged. You sense your unique place and perspective in the world, and you take joy in sharing your ideas and feelings through whatever medium you can, whether painting on canvas, singing on stage, or thwacking away on a keyboard. At work, you're likely to ask more questions, spend more time forming your own opinions, and share more of your ideas with others. You also have a greater sense of play when taking on new challenges and projects, since each brings new opportunities to leave your singular mark on the world.

Neurologically, being more in touch with your creative side means you're activating the right side of your brain more. This is the hemisphere that tends to process more big-picture thinking and concepts, interpret how things are said, tune in to your body and emotions, synthesize unique elements into a greater whole, visualize the future, and so on. I also think of it as the *disruptive* seat of the mind, allowing us to deconstruct and rethink how things are, act against the conventional or socially accepted wisdom, and recast and re-create ourselves and the world around us.

This is a chapter about getting back in touch with your creative side and becoming more intelligent and strategic in creatively expressing who you are in the world. The stakes are probably higher than you imagine. If you lose touch with your creative expression, you lose touch with what is uniquely you—and, thus, you lose connection with self. Activating your drive for creative expression is one of the fastest strategies to finding happiness and fulfillment. It also happens to be the best way to guarantee your future employment.

The Future of the World of Work

Harsh news from the New Economy: if you can't tap into your creative self and fully express your ideas and unique talents, strengths, and perspectives, you'll likely soon find yourself unemployed.

The world really has changed to favor a new kind of worker, what I call the "creative collaborator." The person who can be individually creative at work yet also socially adept and tuned in when collaborating with others is the one who wins.

Don't mistake my tone for the creative platitudes of a self-proclaimed "maverick." All the data we have on today's workforce supports this creative bent, and I'm certainly not the first to note the trend.

In *The Rise of the Creative Class*, author Richard Florida notes that in 1900, less than 10 percent of American workers were doing creative work. Most people did fairly repetitive and routine work on farms or in factories. But routinized physical labor was long ago replaced by the mental heavy lifting of the knowledge economy. By the early 2000s, nearly one-third of the workforce was doing creative work. The creative engineers, artists, scientists, designers, and knowledge-based workers started accounting for nearly *half* of all wage and salary income in the United States—nearly $2 trillion. The creative class was driving more of the economy than manufacturing and services combined.

By 2005, Daniel Pink, author of *A Whole New Mind*, declared the creative type the rulers of the new world, saying, "The future belongs to a very different kind of person with a very different kind of mind—creators and empathizers, pattern recognizers, and meaning makers. These people—artists, inventors, designers, storytellers, caregivers, consolers, big picture thinkers—will now reap society's richest rewards and share its greatest joys."

None of this is to say that left-brainers must be left behind—they simply must be well-rounded. Thinking logically and sequentially and excelling at analysis, language, and list-making will always be critical to success. It's just that these alone are no longer sufficient in a world so heavily driven by design and innovation. Your smarts have to be matched by your storytelling ability so that you can better connect and communicate your ideas. Your functional designs have to be elevated by aesthetic design so that people see the beauty in what you create and sell. Your linear thinking had better be applied to a bigger vision and picture that resonates emotionally with those you lead. In short, you need to bring a creative sensibility to everything you do at work.

Even today's technology titans are but platforms for self-expression. Gone are the days when technology was functionally driven and popular because of what it enabled you to do or achieve. Spreadsheets, word processing, PowerPoint—the stuff of Microsoft—used to rule the world. No longer. Today what makes technology cool and an economic powerhouse is less about what it enables you to do than about how it helps you express yourself. In fact, while most tech commentators think that connection and community drive software's success, they are missing a deeper reality. What's interesting is that all modern-day technology platforms—Facebook and YouTube, for instance—have thrived not just because of their community functions, but in large part because they came at a time when the world was starving for platforms that let people share themselves with the world. The social-media sphere isn't actually driven by a desire to connect and gather fans and followers as much as by a deeper need to express ourselves creatively. Posting quotes, reflections on our experiences, or impressions we have of places we visit or things we see are distinctly creative endeavors. The bonus of social media is that it lets us express ourselves creatively to the world, but the connection function of social media is just that: a bonus. Creative expression is the driver of Facebook, Twitter, You-Tube, and all other modern platforms.

The workplace's sea change toward creativity has major implications for your work life. The old social compact of "do your job well and you'll keep it" died in the early 1990s, when downsizing, optimizing, and outsourcing overtook the world of business strategy. Keeping a job today isn't about doing a "good job" or being the smartest or most pleasant to work with. Nor is it about simply organizing and managing information or people. Now you have to be an innovator, adding new value and competitive advantage through your creative input and collaborations. If you're not creative and collaborative, no one listens to you, and you quickly find yourself marginalized, tasked with the mundane, or, more likely, laid off or seeing your work outsourced. Your role at work is now fundamentally judged by how well you create new ideas, tools, technologies, content, and campaigns that help your clients and coworkers tap into their highest potential or express themselves more fully.

The good news about all this is that the demand for creativity at work is allowing us to bring an entirely new level of autonomy, voice, and contribution to our daily lives. When you get to put your own personal touch on a project, you feel that you are making a real impact. Seeing your ideas resonate with others and come to fruition is one of the greatest rewards of work, and the creative collaboration at play in modern organizations makes that very thing possible.

Clearly, creative expression is important in both our personal and professional lives, and if we're going to feel fully expressed (and win in the New Economy), we've got to get serious about it. Let's begin by assessing just how much you've been creatively expressing yourself.

Activator #1: Amplify Creative Expression in All Areas of Your Life

To help you realize just how creative you are and, in turn, help you inject more creativity into your life, it's first important to understand that everything you do is an act of self-expression and creativity. The way you write your emails, dress for work, or decorate your home is an act of expression. Our job here is to figure out how much creative voice you are putting into those acts.

If you look around your home and think about your work and can't see *you* there, then we're in trouble.

Let's begin with a simple five-part test I've given to thousands of clients, which I call simply the Creative Expression Quiz. On a scale of zero to ten, with zero meaning none and ten meaning the most, score how much you see and sense your personal style, voice, and imprint in several areas of your life. Here we go.

Creative Expression Quiz

- *Home:* How much "you" do you see and sense at your home? Is your unique style all over your home? Did you have a hand in picking the wall colors, the furniture, the lighting, the layout? Does your home really reflect who you are as a person? Consider all these questions and give yourself a score.

- *Work:* How much "you" do you see and sense at work? Is your work space uniquely you, featuring items, photographs, or design chosen by you? Do you feel that your coworkers have a sense of your individual strengths, style, and personality? Are your signature style and creative input all over the past five projects you worked on? Consider all these questions and give yourself a score.

- *Intimate Relationship:* How much do you see and sense your voice and values in your intimate relationship with your spouse or partner? Do the two of you do things that you enjoy and choose to do? Does your partner understand your values, communication style, quirks, and life ambitions? Do you feel that you bring flare and a fun independence to your relationship? Consider all these questions and give yourself a score.

- *Friendships:* How much do you see and sense your voice and values in your friendships? Do you do things with your friends that you enjoy and choose to do? Do your friends understand your values, communication style, quirks, and life ambitions? Do you feel that you bring flare and a fun independence to your friendships? Consider all these questions and give yourself a score.

- *Leisure:* How much "you" do you see and sense in your life of leisure outside your work life, family life, and social life? Do you read the books you would like to read? Are you pursuing hobbies that make you feel that you're expressing who you uniquely are? Consider all these questions and give yourself a score.

- *Contributions:* How much "you" do you see and sense in the ways you are contributing to the world in general? Do you feel you are leaving your unique imprint on the world? Do you sense that your work and volunteering reflect the essence of who you are? Do you feel you are adding a distinct voice and contribution to your community and the world at large? Consider all these questions and give yourself a score.

Now add all your scores from the categories above. If your over-all score isn't forty-five or above, then your life is lacking something deeply important: *you*. A lower score than that means you're not expressing who you are in some of the most important domains of your life. It would also suggest that you're likely cheating yourself and those around you of the joy of hearing from and knowing the real, authentic, unique, and creative you. If this is your score level, then it's time to bring a renewed commitment to living and creatively expressing who you really are. The world wants to see more of *you* in your life. There are more than 7 billion people on the planet. Among them, you are unique. Live that.

I've also noticed that the higher the score, the happier the per-son. This makes a lot of sense. How creative we feel in everyday life has a lot to do with how expressed and fulfilled we are in life. Luckily, there's nothing really tricky about moving the needle of creativity in each of these domains—it just takes a little focus and consistency. Go back to the Creative Expression Quiz now and turn it into a Creative Expression Planner by writing out each of the categories and ask-ing yourself how you can bring more creativity to that area of your life. Take time to do this now before moving on. You'll see that just the act of creating these ideas will energize you, revealing one of the great joys of this drive—just *thinking* of how to be more creative in life can make you feel energized, engaged, and enthusiastic.

Activator #2: Study People and Design

I've been blessed to work with many of the world's most creative artists, singers, actors, authors, luminaries, and designers, and I've found that while they are each incredibly unique, they all had the same approach to developing their creativity. They were all avid peo-ple watchers and design lovers.

While many people think of highly creative people as lone artists, designers, or geniuses toiling away alone in their studios and offices, it turns out that creatives are incredibly social people whose creativity literally depends on their interactions with the world. This is why nearly every creative in the world would give you the exact same advice if you were to ask him or her, "How do I become more creative?" The answer would be, "Go watch people and explore the world."

I once worked for a major clothing retailer that was struggling to be seen as more creative in the marketplace. To help its executives unleash creativity, it brought in one of the world's most famed design firms to advise its executives. Here's what the designers told them to do: *go shopping*. Really. The design firm suggested the retail executives get out in the "field" (malls), watch people shop, take notes, ask customers questions about why they bought what they were buying, notice what they themselves liked and didn't like, and then go back to their offices and brainstorm and start designing. For this advice, the design firm charged hundreds of thousands of dollars.

The world's most creative people are, at their cores, people watchers. They know that the spark of creative expression often comes to us not out of solitude but out of social inspiration. That's why they're intrigued by how people behave, interact, communicate, use products, work, shop, worship, and organize. In this sense, they're like anthropologists. You can learn a lot from them. If you want to become more creatively expressed in life, start watching people as a *practice*, paying close attention to how others creatively express themselves. Notice what they like and don't like, express and don't express. Sometimes, just paying attention to people helps us notice new things within ourselves.

Not all people-watching is equally able to spur our own creative expression. You might find people-watching at the mall or the airport as a source of inspiration, but if you want the greatest amount of creative inspiration, do what the world's most creative people do: engage

in the arts. Watching a professional dance troupe can make you want to dance. Seeing an artist's gallery can make you want to pick up a brush. Hearing a great musician can make you want to take up an instrument. While not all these examples may be true for you specifically, there's no question that being around the creativity exuded in the arts engages and develops your brain's right hemisphere and your mirror neurons. What you see is what you feel like, so watching the arts makes you feel more artistic. And that can only be a good thing.

When our creative energy in life seems to be flatlining, it's important to remember all this. If you ever hit that point, get out of your house and go engage with the world again. Remember, genius loves company.

I learned this lesson when writing this book. After several creative successes, including a number one *New York Times* bestselling book, I fell into the trap of seeking solitude in creating my next work. I thought, *If I can just get away from all the insanity of the world, then I'll be able to think better*. But being in solitude, I quickly found myself unable to write creatively. Then I happened to talk with another very successful author who reminded me of the importance of getting out into the world to engage my social, curious mind. The very next day, I started going out to lunch at a popular café and arted people-watching, visited a local museum, and called some nds to tell and hear a few good stories. That night, I wrote better had in weeks. This became the mantra of healing my brain and after my concussion: "connecting your brain means g with people and the world."

s today: Pry open your daily newspaper and see what's wn this weekend. Go catch a show, listen to a symphony, take a course. Get into the local art scene, if for no n to surround yourself with creatives outside your while observing acts of creative expression, ask

yourself, *What do I think of that? What does this inspire me to think or do or become?*

Since you're going to be paying more attention to other people and getting out and about in the world again, also start paying attention to how *things* are designed. Notice how your phone is shaped, your car's interior is laid out, your work space is structured—and ask yourself, *Why is it so, and could this be better designed for form and function?* Leonardo da Vinci is said to have asked his apprentices similar questions to engage their curiosity and creativity.

You already have a design mind-set. When you rearrange your living room, change the layout of a presentation, match your outfits, or envision a new way a product could look, you are designing. It's in pushing this natural strength into a more conscious and consistent realm that you begin to feel more fully alive. So, pick up a few design magazines, update the art or furnishings in your home, or keep a journal and note what you like or don't like about the design of the products you interact with every day.

Activator #3: Create More, Share More

Don't just be an observer of creativity, always looking to others and things—translate your inspiration into real works. Creativity isn't ju about ideas; it's about physical form. The idea is the spark, the p cal form the outcome. Having an idea for a book isn't creat just a thought. Writing the book and putting pen to pap page is creative expression. Real creativity ends up

Often, the things we create define our legacy. judge the great artistic and business legends of what they have created. We are in awe of Leo just as we are in awe of Steve Jobs's prod just something about us that gives icon tangible forms productively over the

But building a legacy isn't always easy, so a convenient excuse for many is, *Well, I'm not that creative.* Creativity, though, isn't a trait; it's a discipline. Those who say they are not creative are often those who are averse to the hard work of transforming a good idea into something truly magnificent.

I like to remind people that creativity also isn't a spark; it's a slog. Every artist, inventor, designer, writer, or other creative in the world will talk about his work being an iterative experience. He'll start with one idea, shape it, move it, combine it, break it, begin anew, discover something within himself, see a new vision, go at it again, test it, share it, fix it, break it, hone it, hone it, hone it. This might sound like common sense, but it's not common practice, and that's why so many people are terribly uncreative—they're not willing to do the work required to create something that's beautiful, useful, desirable, celebrated. No masterpiece was shaped or written in a day. It's a long slog to get something right. This knowledge and willingness to iterate is what makes the world's most creative people so creative (and successful).

I'm guessing you've had creative dreams that you've let go of too early. You wanted to sing but didn't win the competition, and so you gave up. You wanted to paint, but no one liked your first attempts, so you stopped. You wanted to dance, dress more colorfully, write more forcefully, speak with more fire, invent something big, or redesign a process entirely—but you stopped expressing yourself along the way. You had the spark, and maybe you began, but you didn't *slog it through*. But what if expressing yourself and following your creative spark to completion would have led to something more magnificent than you ever imagined? I say it's time to reengage your creative spirit and light it up and follow it through thick and thin, through iteration after iteration.

That's why I say it's time to create something again. If you have an idea for a new fashion design, go get a sewing machine and manifest the design in real life. If you've ever had any burning desire to invent, design, sculpt, create, develop, or share, *go do it* in real life. Bring the idea into the physical realm and enjoy the process. It will enliven you.

Finally, don't keep all this creativity to yourself. It turns out that one of the greatest ways to activate creativity in your life is to *share more*. Share your works with others, get their feedback. Also important, start telling more stories about what fascinates you in the world. Explain to people why you like the brands and products in your life, and ask them why they like or don't like theirs. It's in sharing and gathering perspective from others that we discover our own preferences and personalities in life. This is an important point. So many people want to find their unique voices in the world, but voice is not something you "find"; it's something you *share*. You don't walk into a room, look around, and say, "Oh, there's my unique voice in the world." Rather, you walk into the room, talk to a bunch of people, and, *in sharing*, discover and communicate traits and truths about the essence of who you are. That's what the most fulfilling and energizing kind of creative expression is all about—sharing the essence of who you are with the world.

CHARGE POINTS

1. To show more of me and express myself more creatively at home and at work, I will . . .

2. To be more inspired by people and design in my life, I could start . . .

3. The next thing I'm going to physically create and share with the world will be . . .

Chapter Eleven

THE DRIVE FOR
CONTRIBUTION

*We make a living by what we get, we make a life
by what we give.*

—Winston Churchill

I just want to matter. Maybe if I were doing something more important than what I'm doing now, I would feel happier."

She's a thirty-eight-year-old bank manager with as many employees as she's had birthdays. She's slurring her words—a result of the
cucumber margaritas she keeps spilling on the bar. She has a few
years on me, but she's on the hunt, and it seems that tonight I was
supposed to be her quarry. She had no idea what she was in for.

Yes, I am the victim of a cougar attack at the moment, and neither my client nor my wife is around to rescue me. Unfortunately,
I'm a sucker, and my face must show it. I'm terribly fascinated by
people, and when they start conversations with me I'm almost
always trapped for too long. This woman—Janie, she tells me—was
asking what I do for a living. I kept my response brief and polite and
intended to leave, but she started talking about all the motivational
speakers her company hires to come in and speak at their conferences. Within minutes, she was telling me everything that was wrong

with her life. At the moment, it's that she doesn't feel she is making much of a difference in the world. She feels she might not have found her calling yet and maybe never will.

It's not that I feel I have to inspire everyone I meet, but I do have this deep belief in fate and the universe's higher reason for making people's paths cross. I believe that if I meet you, there's a reason, and I ought to try to figure it out and contribute in some way to your life, even if it's just to give you a brief respite from your day so you can laugh or reconnect with your strength or your dream. It's just the way I am.

So back to Janie. She has a problem, she says, with all these motivational speakers, one of whom she mistakenly thinks I am. (I'd prefer "high-performance trainer and strategist," but what are you going to do?)

"Every time I hear them," she says, "all I hear is that I'm probably not a good enough person and I'm definitely not living a high enough purpose. I wonder if it's true. You know? Maybe I'm not making a real difference, and it bugs me. But I do like what I do. I'm not feeding a bunch of kids in Africa or wherever, but I like what I do."

"I'm glad you like what you do, Janie. Keep at it, then. Someone will be inspired by your example of loving what you do, and that's enough. Good night."

I stand up to leave, and she sinks her claws into my arm. "Are you being condescending, young man?" she asks, pointing her finger at me and making a face that I'm not sure how to interpret.

"No. I'm not. Hear me now. Listen. It inspires people to see you loving what you do, no matter what it is. That's contribution enough to the world. Good for you. Now, if you'll excuse me, good night." I pull away from her and leave the bar, thinking nothing more of it.

Two days later, I'm back in the area, catching a cab to the airport. I realize I don't have any cash, and I see an ATM on the corner. Sliding my card into the slot, I happen to glance in the bank branch window, and there I see the cougar—er, Janie—from the other night. She's talking with an employee and wearing much more professional clothing than the other night.

I understand that coincidences happen, but when I meet a random person and see her two days in a row, I pay attention. *I hear you, Fate*, I say to myself, and I walk into the branch. My goals are to get cash from the teller and see where this moment leads me.

When I walk to the teller counter, I make eye contact with Janie, but she doesn't seem to notice me. I say to the teller, "That woman over there—she looks like she's the boss or something?"

"Yes, that's Jane, our bank manager. She's awesome."

"Oh? What makes her awesome?"

"Well, look around at this bank. It's the cleanest and nicest and brightest in town. All my coworkers are awesome, and Jane is always challenging us to get better."

"So you like your job?"

"I *love* it. I'm part of something here. I know it's not a big-time job like a lot of the customers I meet have. I used to work in the back office. Oh, my God, I was terribly shy. I mean, *really* shy. And all I did was do a bunch of paperwork back there and cry half the day, worrying my husband would get killed over there—he's deployed in Iraq. But Jane said, 'You need to be out and about in the world, and you need to talk out all that stress, girl.' So she trained me herself, and now I get to do this. Jane has inspired all of us to actually talk with people and enjoy our relationships with people. It's been good for me, for everybody."

When I finish my conversation with the teller and have my money in hand, I walk over to Jane, who is still talking to an employee. As I near her, I don't sense that she recognizes me.

"Hi, I'm just a random guy coming in," I say, "and I wanted to share something with you. That woman over there, the teller—do you see her?"

Jane and the employee nod.

"Well, I just wanted to let you know she was incredibly pleasant and helpful." I turn to Jane directly and try to speak with depth so she'll know I'm meaning what I say. "I also wanted you to know that she acknowledged you as someone who inspires her and has helped her cope with her husband's being gone. She says you run the best branch in the city, and from the look of things here, I believe her. She's really impressed by you, and you've made a huge difference in that woman's life. You really matter, and you've done a great job here. I just wanted to say good for you and thanks for what you do."

Jane is genuinely surprised and blushes. She shakes my hand and thanks me for being a customer. I can tell she doesn't recognize me.

As I turn to leave, I say, "Good for you. Inspiring that girl and doing good work here is just as good as feeding the kids in Africa."

I hail a cab just as it's passing in front of the bank and hurry to jump in. As I do, the bank door opens and Jane walks out, looking to her left and right. I can tell she finally remembered who I am. She sees me sitting down in the car.

She yells, "Thank you! Very motivational! I hear you!"

• • •

At our deepest depths rises a drive to contribute. We want to know that we've given of ourselves and played a significant part in shaping the world around us. Our desires to add value, give to others, express ourselves, create unique things, and join groups and organizations are often all in hopes of making our mark on the world and making some kind of difference. It's this drive to give and to matter that fuels our highest personal ambitions as well as our remarkable ability to be selfless.

When we feel as though we're contributing to the world, we gain a profound sense of meaning and purpose. In fact, contribution itself is the source of meaning and purpose in our lives. If we've contributed something significant to the world, we feel that our time here was meaningful, that it mattered. And if we know what we are contributing now and planning to contribute in the future, then we feel we are living a life of purpose. Sadly, many people, like Janie, are truly unaware of how much they contribute.

Strip away our sense of contribution from us, though, and you strip away our meaning and purpose. That's why, when we don't feel that we're contributing, we feel so lost and unfulfilled. We sense that nothing really matters or, worse, that *we* don't matter. This is what happens when we don't *feel* that we're contributing. When that feeling is a reality and we really *aren't* contributing, then we lose an important sense of pride that comes with knowing we've given something significant. We also lose our connection with others, because they don't feel we're playing our part, adding value, or being helpful.

With so much on the line, it's helpful to know what we mean by the word "contribution" and to understand how we can use it more strategically in our lives to experience the sense of meaning and purpose we desire and deserve. What does it really mean to contribute? When I ask audiences from around the world this question, the most frequent answers sound like basic maxims of motivation: "Make a difference. Leave a legacy. Do something important. Share your gifts and abilities. Leave things better than you found them." All these mantras and most people's responses ultimately involve one thing: *giving*.

Indeed, contribution is generally defined as "playing a significant part in" some kind of common or collective cause or endeavor. So contributing in life is akin to giving significantly to something, whether to work, a cause, a group, or an individual. That's obvious.

What's not obvious is that not all methods of contribution are created equal, and that not all giving leads to real impact in the world or to a sense of personal engagement and fulfillment. In fact, giving can have little whatever to do with stirring our drive for contribution— or even happiness, for that matter.

Of course, this can sound sacrilegious to a bleeding heart. "Giving is good" is the mantra of our modern society. But then, why are there so many unhappy volunteers in the world? I'm sure you've seen them, grudgingly doing their good works. I sure have. I spend a fair amount of time in the nonprofit world, and I've met thousands of volunteers who are giving of their time and energy but who clearly lack a smile or any obvious personal enjoyment from the activity at hand. I've even seen volunteers who are downright rude and mean to those they serve. Yes, they are "giving" and contributing to an important cause, but, no, they aren't happy. Likewise, I'm sure you've met *plenty* of people who give and contribute tremendously but are happy.

This is where it becomes helpful to begin differentiating between various types of giving and to notice how they affect our overall drive for contribution. We can think of giving as being one of two varieties: *giving of* and *giving to*.

Activator #1: Give of Yourself (and Give Yourself Credit While You're at It)

In the first, we give *of* ourselves with full expression and effort in our everyday lives, though that giving is not necessarily tied to giving *to* any cause, group, or individual at all. By giving the best of ourselves to everything we do, we exert our highest and strongest selves, and *doing that alone* can make us feel that we are contributing. Here's what I mean. If I'm a tennis player and exert my full effort in a match, enlisting all my strengths, talents, and abilities, I will likely feel I am giving of myself. Thus, I feel that I am activating my drive for contribution. It doesn't even require that I feel I am contributing *to* the game of tennis, *to* the fans, or even *to* the moment. Just giving *of myself* can activate my sense of personal contribution.

This sounds a little odd—almost as if I'm taking a selfish perspective on contribution. But after coaching and training and getting the live feedback of tens of thousands of people, I've come to realize that contributing to the world doesn't always have to be a social affair. I bring this to light because too many people think of contributing as simply giving *to* something specific, so they never feel that they contribute to the world except when a Girl Scout shows up at the door hawking cookies. Ours is a society that has falsely assumed that contribution must mean giving *to* some specific cause rather than simply giving *of* our best selves. *Thus, too many people don't recognize the fact that simply being who they are is contributing significantly to the world.*

What if simply living your truth, being your best, and fully expressing your strengths, talents, and abilities at whatever you do were sufficient to contribute to the world? I say it is, and we must not overlook the fact that being our best ultimately inspires others and can and does indeed make an impact.

Steve Jobs didn't need to give *to* anything in particular to contribute immensely to the world. Jobs reportedly didn't do things with an eye toward giving *to* the tech industry, the computer market, or perhaps even to consumers (though a relentless focus on the customer experience made him famous). Unlike many billionaires, he didn't form a public nonprofit (though his wife did and does) or have an interest in publicly showing off what he gave to. You don't know Steve Jobs for what he gave to charities or certain causes or audiences. You know him for having been who he was fully: a creative guy who wanted to design and build better software, computers, stores, and mobile devices. He affected the world by doing what he did with excellence. For that, he contributed, he mattered, and he will be missed.

This point can't be underscored enough. Consider, for example, the artists—the singers, dancers, writers, designers, and so on—who may not be creating with an eye toward giving to anything in particular but, rather, with the intention of living their truth and following their creative expression. Perhaps the singer who sells millions of copies of her album has contributed something to her musical genre and to millions of fans worldwide, but she may not have viewed it that way. She was simply giving of her best efforts in her creative endeavor. "Contribution" as we think of it came later. Personally, I've been inspired by hundreds of people who were just going about their lives as authentic, caring people. They made a huge difference in my life, though they likely didn't think they were "doing contribution."

You have an extraordinary ability to contribute to the world by bringing the best in you to bear in any endeavor. Give of yourself fully to your creative endeavors. Recognize that as a contribution, and you just might find yourself feeling that you are living a more meaningful and purposeful life.

Finally, before we hop into another kind of contribution, *giving to*, it's important that you give yourself credit for all the things you've already done in life. Sometimes we forget to integrate our own personal contributions to the world into our identity. This is important, because unlike other human drives, contribution brings up a lot of guilt. People simply don't feel they're contributing enough to their families, coworkers, and greater community. This is especially true in today's überbusy and connected world, where they don't have time to address many pressing issues and yet are constantly reminded of them. Take some time to complete the following sentences. Then, from now on, every time you finish a project or get a compliment for a contribution you've made to the world, take a moment to let it all in. Allow satisfaction to enter your heart. You matter.

- The ways I've contributed to and made a difference in my family's life this past year include . . .
- When I think of my best friends, I know I've made an impact in their lives in these ways: . . .

- A creative project I've finished in the past few years that I never really gave myself credit for was . . .
- If I started giving myself more credit for the ways I really do give and contribute in this world, my life would change in these ways: . . .

It's time you finally allowed yourself to sense the impact and contributions you've made in the world. You have made a difference in this world, regardless of whether it's as large or lasting as you would hope. Recognizing your impact isn't an activity I suggest just so you can pat yourself on the back (though I think that is a good thing for most people). It's so you can sense a grander meaning and purpose to all that you've experienced in life. Your contributions have added and will continue to add up to something. It's time to take account of them so that you finally give yourself the credit you deserve. You are a contribution to this world. Whether or not you ever give grand amounts of money to a cause, start a nonprofit, or volunteer decades of your life, you have already contributed. Know that.

Activator #2: Give to (Deeply Meaningful Contribution Experiences)

Another kind of giving is the variety of giving *to* others and broader causes outside ourselves with the direct intention of making an impact. You can give your time, energy, effort, resources, skills, connections, attention, and love *to* your team, your company, your family, your favorite nonprofit. While giving *of* is really about mobilizing our internal resources for our own sakes, which often ultimately leads to an impact in the world, giving *to* is all about mobilizing our resources with the specific intent to contribute to something directly and specifically. You give to a person, cause, or group because you have an eye toward what specific impact you can make and how you will feel afterward. Giving *to* is a more strategic, "aimed" approach at contribution, and it's just as powerful.

This is the type of giving that most of the world recognizes and rewards, and for good reason. Giving to endeavors that you find deeply meaningful, with an intent to make an impact, *is* a direct path to meaning and happiness. But note the operative phrase: *endeavors that you find deeply meaningful.*

Here is where this type of giving often goes awry. People find themselves volunteering for projects or causes at random without the criterion of "deeply meaningful," and they end up deeply disappointed in the experience. I'm sure you've been there. You got excited about giving to a cause, you got involved and gave of your time, energy, or money, yet you never sensed you had a real impact or felt the soulful buzz of doing good.

For example, I might resonate more with a cause whose mission is about feeding starving children than with one that helps kids learn to sing. But if the first cause has me doing nothing but washing dishes (something I dislike), and the second has me teaching (something I enjoy), then there is little doubt that over time I will find the latter more meaningful. That is to say, *choosing the right giving activity matters just as much as choosing the right cause.* Never forget that, since it also echoes much of what we've discussed in the book so far: activities that we find novel, challenging, socially connected, and personally meaningful make us happy.

I've also learned that not all giving experiences—whether to causes, projects, groups, family, community, or something or someone else—are created equal. In fact, deeply meaningful giving experiences are set apart by five factors—which I have termed, in a blinding flash of creativity, the Five Contribution Fulfillment Factors. Knowing these factors may serve as a handy filter for you in deciding what to give to in the future. It will also provide insights into which contributions become the most meaningful to you personally and the most beneficial to society at large.

First, to feel that you are truly contributing to a cause or to the greater world, you must have the ability to leverage your strengths in some type of creative activity. To use a term from the previous chapter, having an opportunity for *creative expression* is critical to finding a giving experience deeply satisfying and meaningful. For example, if you have a strong talent for design, look for design opportunities in whatever you are giving to. Leveraging your strengths in this way is important, because no matter how much you care for a cause or are committed to a giving experience, if you can't bring your unique voice, talents, or perspective to the experience, you will leave or else engage only halfheartedly.

There's more. Not only must you be able to activate your creativity in the giving experience, you must also get to see your creative works come to fruition. That is, your creative contribution must have a chance at seeing the light of day. There's nothing worse than contributing to a project at work and never getting to see any of your ideas or efforts actually cross the finish line. If everything you give to an experience ends up in the garbage can or on a dusty shelf or gets used in a way you don't see, you never get to experience the sense of pride that truly activates your drive for significant contribution.

Here's an easy test to figure out if you found your last contribution deeply satisfying and meaningful: Did you produce any creative works during the experience? Was there tangible evidence that you had a hand in shaping the results of whatever you were engaged in? If not, you probably didn't sense you were contributing or that the experience was worthwhile.

Second, the most meaningful experiences in giving and contributing *always* involve mentoring others. Talk to any teacher in the world, and when he talks about seeing his students' eyes light up, you'll understand why he finds his experience of giving to children so rewarding. There's just nothing like teaching or guiding someone who has less experience or perspective than you.

Oddly, though most people know this truth, they don't use it as a criterion for selecting how they will contribute. When deciding on a new job, project, or volunteer experience, few people are strategic enough to ask, "Will this opportunity guarantee my ability to mentor others?" Yet this is precisely the question we must learn to ask if we want to feel we are contributing meaningfully to the world. Teaching, coaching, or mentoring puts our sense of contribution into hyperdrive like nothing else in the world, period.

Third, satisfying contribution experiences let us see the *direct social impact* of our efforts. If you volunteer in a soup kitchen and you're stuck in the back unloading crates of produce and never get to see someone's face light up when he tastes the food, the experience just isn't the same. Your mirror neurons never get to light up with the same joy as those of the person finally filling his belly with tasty, nourishing food. You don't see the appreciation in his face, so you don't feel it in your heart.

If you lead others in contributing to your organization, getting to see the fruition of your work must be a part of every new initiative. How can you ensure that your team gets to see the results of their efforts in the real world? Can you take your people to visit those whose lives they've touched or bring those folks to your people to share how their lives have been changed for the better?

When I talk about seeing the direct social impact of your efforts, I specifically mean seeing and hearing how you've affected *people*. I taught this lesson once to a CEO of a large home-building company. He had rallied hundreds of his people to go build homes in a disadvantaged community ravaged by a recent flood. Like a huge SWAT team, his company descended on the area, tore down flooded homes, and built new ones in a matter of days, then flew out and went back to headquarters. When he was giving me a slide show

of his efforts, full of pictures of his people smiling and building, he shared how disappointed he felt that more people in the company didn't understand what a profound effect they'd had in the community. At that point, I commented that I didn't see any photos of his employees with actual people who would be inhabiting the new homes. *Bang!* A light went off in his head. In their rush to go in and make a difference, they hadn't made a true connection, and therefore they didn't feel they had made a real contribution.

Of course, many die-hard givers will note that my Five Contribution Fulfillment Factors have a transparently selfish bent—they are focused on our own internal sense of enjoyment and fulfillment. That's a terribly self-seeking approach to giving and contributing to the world, no? After all, shouldn't we all be much more selfless, contributing our time and attention not to efforts that bring *us* joy but rather to those in need?

The short answer is, well, no. First, we live in an age when there are literally *millions* of important and pressing causes around the world. The United States alone has nearly two million nonprofit organizations. How should we all look past our personal interests and magically choose which are the most important and deserving? Is an organization serving fifty battered women in Detroit any more or less important than one serving five hundred in West Africa?

So the question must be this: Where can we make our unique contribution to serve, and where can we do it in a way that keeps us engaged, fulfilled, and most likely to continue serving and making an impact? In the end, isn't the goal of contributing to get involved, stay involved, and have a beneficial impact?

In proposing a framework for thinking about how you contribute, I'm certainly not suggesting that all your giving experiences will be fun and uplifting, nor should that be the singular goal. Contributing often means rolling up your sleeves, getting dirty, and doing

things you would rather not do. It means taking on tasks that might make you uncomfortable. This is the stuff that makes life feel so engaging: doing new things, taking risks, working hard, being challenged, connecting with new people, fighting for something important no matter how arduous the journey.

Still, the world is full of half-interested, halfhearted would-be contributors playing at quarter speed. We're not going to shift the planet if we don't engage ourselves and others in finding fulfilling ways to contribute. I hope my framework can help to that end.

Finally, a discussion on giving wouldn't be complete without addressing financial contributions. If you are blessed with abundance in this area of your life, donating money to your favorite causes is a great complement to giving of your time and effort. It's widely known that donating to an organization you are passionate about is important if it is to be a fulfilling giving experience. So heed that advice and target causes you really care about.

As I've met people from around the globe, I've continually found that many people simply don't know what to give to. They don't have a deep passion for one cause or another, and even with my framework above I know they may struggle to find one, especially when it comes to figuring out where to give money. To those with deeper pockets but without a deep passion for a specific cause, I suggest an alternative approach I call "fate funding." I've shared this idea rather widely now, and everyone I've ever introduced to it loves it, especially if they haven't "found their thing" to give to.

Fate funding comes from my belief that on the road of life, there is a reason that other people's paths cross our own. I believe, for example, that it's no coincidence that I meet someone at work who has lost his wife to breast cancer and is now running a marathon in her honor and seeking a hundred-dollar contribution from the guys at the office. Fate placed someone with a need in my path, and con-

tributing to his need and cause—even if it's not a cause I am directly tied to—is more rewarding than contributing to a random cause I found online. Further, I don't believe in contributing to causes or projects; I believe in investing in and serving people. So I write the hundred-dollar check because that's what fate has decided to ask of me, even though I've never directly known someone who had breast cancer nor would that be a cause I would one day randomly go out, research, and give to. Fate funding—it means giving to those whom fate has placed right in front of us who are in need or have a cause they are deeply passionate about.

At this point in my life, a majority of my giving is now fate funding, and I'm happy to share that I've never felt so enlivened about making financial contributions to causes. I'm also excited to share just how powerful others have found this approach. People report feeling more connected to their immediate communities and circle of influence, and they now see the fruits of their giving in more direct and meaningful ways than they ever imagined. Fate funding might not be for all people, especially those who've already picked a cause to be loyal to or who simply don't have the funds to give to seemingly random people or causes that enter their spheres of influence. Still, what if we all just gave a little more to the people who cross our paths and have a need or a passion that could benefit from our generosity?

Activator #3: Mentor, Mentor, Mentor

As I've eluded to, there's nothing more powerful in activating your drive for contribution than mentoring others.

I like to think of mentoring as a responsibility and a privilege on the road of life. No matter what mile marker you are walking past at this point in life, there are thousands of people behind you who would love to learn how you made it so far so fast. Kids want to know how you finished school alive and found a decent job. Coworkers want to know how to be better at what they do. The downtrodden just want to know how to keep walking.

Something magical happens in a mentorship relationship, whether it's a formal relationship arranged at work or in the community through friends, or a great organization such as Big Brothers Big Sisters. What I like about it is, there's this point where maybe you need those you mentor as much as they need you. The mentorship casts you as a role model, and engaging in that role inspires you to call forth the best in you. All your highest virtues and beliefs start emanating from you because you want to help others soar. Over time, the more you mentor someone, the deeper the relationship becomes, and in this person right there in front of you, you get to see your influence and impact. In this way, mentoring is similar to parenthood—you are granted the gift of watching someone grow. But unlike parenthood, this person is unattached to you in some ways. He or she doesn't live with you, doesn't have to listen to you, has less exposure to you than your kids do. So you really have to make your time with the person count, and this is something you realize every time you go to meet with him or her, which is why those in a mentoring relationship often say it is the most presence-filled relationship they have.

And for those who think mentoring is just for a bunch of retired softies, think again. The work I'm most known for is my Experts Academy brand and *The Millionaire Messenger*, which is a distillation of the big picture of that brand. The premise of Experts Academy is simple:

- Your life story, your knowledge, and your message—what you know from experience and want to share with the world—have greater importance and market value than you ever dreamed.

- You are here to make a difference in this world, and the best way to do that is to use your knowledge and experience (on any topic, in any industry) to help others succeed.
- You can get paid for sharing advice and how-to information that helps others succeed, and in the process you can build a very lucrative business and a profoundly meaningful life.

With these three premises, I've helped millions of people worldwide realize the meaning and market value of their wisdom and experience. I've shown them that they can have a career, not just a retirement activity, in guiding others to improve their lives or get ahead in any field. There's no reason at all that you can't contribute to the world with your wisdom and, at the same time, get paid for it. I think this is actually the next evolutionary step in the working world: profit and purpose can mix in a delightfully service-driven way when we share with others what we've learned, researched, or proven on the road of life. We can package our wisdom and how-to advice (on any subject and in any field) into online training programs and courses or via more traditional methods such as books, speeches, seminars, coaching, and consulting. We can make our impact with what we know—and, yes, we can get paid for it, too.

I mention this here because I don't think we have to draw such a hard line between our work and our mentorship activities. They can be one and the same in our modern world. Profit and purpose are no longer mutually exclusive terms. Just like Janie, who is mentoring the tellers at her bank, we all can have an impact at work and in our careers, simply by helping others.

. . .

I'll conclude this chapter with a broader thought about all these Activators. In *Man's Search for Meaning*, Viktor Frankl, a psychologist and Holocaust survivor, suggested that "man's main concern is not to gain pleasure or to avoid pain but rather to see a meaning in his life." If you agree, as I do, then the next logical question would be, "How does one ultimately gauge meaning in one's life?" If life is about meaning, then how will I know if I'm creating it or experiencing it?

The best answer I've found is contribution. At the end of our lives, when we're looking back and wondering about the meaning of it all, we'll wonder if we mattered. To discover the answer, we'll look uniquely to our connections (our loved ones and those we influenced) and to our contributions. But even as we evaluate and reflect on our connections, we're really thinking about what we contributed to those connections. We're wondering whether we gave of ourselves to our relationships, whether we loved fully and openly and honestly. We're wondering whether we gave others the time, attention, acceptance, and affection they deserved from us. We're wondering, essentially, what we contributed to the world and to those around us. In the end, that's how we gauge the meaning of our lives.

CHARGE POINTS

1. I feel I contribute to the world around me by . . .

2. A new and deeply meaningful giving experience I'd like to create is . . .

3. Someone who could use my mentoring is . . .

Chapter Twelve

THE DRIVE FOR
CONSCIOUSNESS

The aim of life is to live, and to live means to be aware,
joyously, drunkenly, serenely, divinely aware.
—HENRY MILLER

Whenter I woke up, Kevin was screaming, "Get out of the car, Brendon! Get out of the car!"

I looked over from my seat on the passenger side of the car. Kevin was scrunched behind the wheel, screaming at me and trying to wrestle his way out of the smashed driver's side window frame. His entire face was covered in blood.

We had rounded the corner going 85 miles per hour. In the United States, that corner would have had a bright yellow sign with a U-shaped arrow, a warning sign indicating a sharp curve is coming up, so you'd better slow down.

But we were in the Dominican Republic on a newly paved road. No signs. And that corner was about to become a turning point in our lives. It turned out to be a blessing. For months I had been depressed and emotionally dead following the breakup with the first woman I ever loved. I was only 19 years old, but I felt adrift, as if my life were over. I was so upset that when an opportunity came to work a summertime job a world away in the Dominican Republic, I jumped at it. Getting out of town to escape my problems and depression was not enough—I had to leave the country.

So there I was in the Dominican Republic with Kevin, a friend from my hometown, helping out an entrepreneur we knew who sold trucking equipment. We were returning from a client's home around midnight. It was a dark, steamy Caribbean night. All the windows were down in our car, and Tom Cochrane's "Life Is a Highway" was blaring on the radio. As we sped down the road, flanked by the dark jungle on either side, with the humid air funneling through the car, I felt a reprieve from my depression. The heaviness of my loneliness and sorrow diminished at the speed of sound. I closed my eyes, trying to forget that my soul felt dead, and I belted out that song at the top of my lungs.

Then Kevin screamed, "Jesus! Brendon, hold on!"

I opened my eyes and saw the headlight beams disappearing ahead of us, off the road into the darkness.

Kevin grabbed the wheel, cranking to the right, desperately trying to negotiate the turn. But it was too late. The car fishtailed, lost traction, and spun off the road. I braced myself and thought, *God, I am not ready*. I did not feel I had fully lived my life yet. It's odd how real and lasting that feeling was. The slow-motion sense created by emergency was in full effect as we slid off the road. An urgent question went through my mind as we skidded into death's doorway: *Did I live?*

Careening off the road, our car smacked into a little retainer wall built for irrigation. We flipped into the air sideways, and I felt the seatbelt forcefully lock me into place. Then I felt a strange weightlessness as we were flipping . . . flipping.

My eyes were closed, but I saw "them" clearly. It was not like I thought it would be. I would have guessed I would see an omniscient viewpoint of my life, just like in the movies, where a reel of memories plays in slow motion, and you see yourself growing up. I didn't see myself now. No little Brendon running around at all.

But I see *them*. My friends and family are standing in front and to the side of me. They are singing around the cake on our living-room table. It is my twelfth birthday party. My mom is crying happily and singing joyously that silly song she sings on our birthdays.

Then a different scene. It's my sister. She is swinging next to me on a swing set. Our eyes meet, and she smiles her big, beautiful smile.

Then more scenes. My life racing before me, experienced through my own eyes. All the scenes are moments when I am surrounded by those I love. I do not feel as if I were in the moments, though they look so real, and I am conscious that I am flipping through the air in slow motion. I think of those I love and those who will miss me. A deep, powerful emotion of regret tugged at my mind: *Did I love?*

The car hit the ground with a body-rattling crash, and I was knocked out.

When I woke, I heard Kevin screaming to get out of the car. I looked over at him from my seat on the passenger side. He was scrunched behind the wheel, screaming at me and trying to get out of the car through the smashed window frame.

He turned to me, and I saw a gaping wound on the right side of his head, and his entire face was covered in blood. "Get out, Brendon!" he said with panic as he slithered through the window.

I didn't know if the car was on fire or what was happening. But Kevin's tone said enough. I looked to my right for escape but the passenger's side window frame was smashed. The whole roof and car was smashed down on top of me. My only escape was a narrow opening in front of me, what used to be the windshield.

I pulled myself through that space, cutting my arms and legs and the skin on my stomach, and I stood, somehow, atop the crumpled white hood of the car. I saw blood oozing from my body, over my feet and sandals, onto the top of the car. I felt dizzy, distant. Slowly, life was draining away and fear slid from my heart to my toes as I realized for the first time that life could really end. A weak and frightened energy then rushed through my body, and I wondered about the point of it all. I struggled through the thought and began to weep. *Did I even matter?*

A dark haze obscured my vision, and I felt I was going to pass out. *This is it*, I thought.

And then a shimmering sparkle at the end of the car's crumpled hood broke my trance. I saw a bright glint, a reflection of light, in my blood that was spilling off the side of the wrecked car. I looked up and saw a magnificent full moon in the darkness of the sky. It was a magical moon, something unlike any I had ever seen before—so close, so big and bright, so beautiful. I felt lifted from the wreckage of my life and deeply connected with the heavens and the waves of blue streaking across in the night sky. There was no pain, no feeling, a nothingness of silence for a moment that I will never forget. And then, slowly, a feeling of centeredness. I was not having an out-of-body experience; in fact, I had never felt more connected to who I was.

I felt a steadiness in my body, and a sense of gratitude washed over me, an appreciation for life that today I still cannot describe. It was as if, in that moment, I looked up to the sky and God had reached down, comforted me, and handed me life's golden ticket— a second chance at life. "Here you go, kid," the moment seemed to say. "You're still alive, you can love again, you can matter. Now, go on and get busy about it, because now you know the clock is ticking."

I remember looking into the sky that night, accepting that ticket, and thinking, *Thank you. Thank you. I will earn this.* A gratitude unlike anything I can describe entered my life, and it has never left.

I felt tears run down my face—the good kind. And for the first time in months, my soul sang.*

• • •

It's been sixteen years since my car accident, and I am still grateful every day that Kevin and I were given life's golden ticket—a second chance. We both survived and are doing well. I think of the accident often, and I have now come to know why it was such a transformative experience in my life. In the space of a few minutes, I was drowned in the depths of my consciousness, awash in thoughts about my own human condition, and, moments later, lifted from my physical body's sensations and connected to a broader consciousness that knew no pain and no bounds. I experienced a shift in my own consciousness about what was important in life, and I decided to be more self-directed in shaping a more meaningful life. Yet I also touched the face of a more magnificent consciousness around me, sensing and knowing for the first time a force beyond my own. I've now learned that the accident helped me experience the dimensions of the two primary ways that philosophers, psychologists, neurologists, and seekers have conceived of the word "consciousness."

In one approach, consciousness has been equated with the mind, that is, with our human-bound capacity to think and be self-aware. *I think; therefore, I am* is an apt expression of this. Neuroscience studies this level of consciousness in search of what brings together our awareness and cohesively shapes the "mind." In *The Feeling of What Happens: Body and Emotion in the Making of Consciousness*, neuroscientist Antonio Damasio, calls consciousness

---

* Text on pages 217–221 is excerpted from Brendon Burchard, *The Millionaire Messenger* (New York: Free Press, 2011), 5–8.

"an organism's awareness of its own self and its surroundings." This focus on our awareness of our internal and external worlds as something experienced primarily by the senses is an approach we can best think of as "thought consciousness."

At a more esoteric level, consciousness has also been defined and described as a nonhuman, perhaps cosmic or divine, unifying energy or force. *God blinked; therefore, I am* expresses this view. "Spiritual" or "heightened" dimensions of consciousness are mostly the study of religious and spiritual seekers who wonder what brings together not just our human awareness but the universe itself. This view sees consciousness as something not just experienced in the mind or apprehended by the bodily senses, but also existing outside the body, as a connection with an energy or entity beyond physical manifestation or our own cognitive understanding. I've come to realize that this conversation is more about "transcendent consciousness."

The drive to experience heightened consciousness is the greatest hallmark of the human species. How do we live at the highest levels of our own human consciousness? How do we transcend them?

We want to establish more control over our thought consciousness while also releasing ourselves from its control so that we may experience a *higher* consciousness. So we want more control over our lives, and, at the same time, many of us sense that we must surrender to the divine. My accident and life since then taught me that we can achieve both. In this chapter, we'll explore both concepts of consciousness and seek to tap into that which leads to our most engaged and energized existence. I've given more time to this drive—this is the longest chapter of the book—because this drive is so rarely discussed in our busy modern lives, yet it remains such a powerful force in all we do.

Activator #1: Focus Your Consciousness

What do we mean when we refer to "human consciousness"? For most of our history, it has meant that which makes us awake, aware, and able to think or manage the mind. Each of these elements creates fascinating questions about our existence and may pave the way toward the heightened experiences we all seek.

Consciousness is usually associated with being alive and in an awakened state. If we are sleeping, we are considered by medical professionals to be "no longer conscious" or simply "unconscious." The same goes for when someone is in a coma or blacked out by trauma or too much alcohol or another drug. According to this definition, when not in a state of wakefulness, you are unable to understand, feel, anticipate, judge, initiate, or be in control of your mental and physical capacities.

Being awake also means you are aware of what is happening around you, which is another hallmark of consciousness. If I am aware of who I am, where I am, what I am doing, why I am doing it, and where I fit within the moment and the social environment, then I am thought to be a fully functioning, conscious being. Self-awareness, in the broadest view, is seen as being a trait of only higher animals.

Of course, the terms "conscious" and "consciousness" are almost always associated with our human ability to think and use our minds. This ability to produce and organize thought into an awareness of self and the context around us distinguishes us from other animals and is something that has fascinated us for ages. We have an uncanny ability to use our minds for cognitive processes such as attention, abstract thinking, impulse control, multitasking, problem solving, and monitoring and initiating thoughts and actions, which is often referred to as "executive control." But how does all this work? And what about the "unconscious" mind—is that really any different from overall human consciousness?

These thorny questions bring up plenty of debate. From philosophical discussions by Descartes and Locke nearly four centuries ago to the latest findings of today's neuroscientists and psychologists, only one thing is for certain: consciousness is tough to pin down. While almost all cultures sense it as an actual thing and feel the drive to explore and enhance it, none of us has ever actually apprehended the thing itself. Neuroscientists can't pry open your brain and say, "There lives your consciousness." We know that *something* enables us to sense the meaning of our emotions and organize our thoughts, but we don't really know what it is. We can't point to it in a brain scan, and even among professionals, everyone defines it differently. What is it that unifies our perception or personhood from all the impulses and activities in the body and brain? When we say that a thought "comes to mind," what mysterious force is creating and admitting that thought into our minds? That great unifier and mysterious force is generally described as "consciousness."

Nailing down this issue of consciousness is important. If we are more conscious or aware of ourselves and our environment, we are simply better attuned and more adaptive. One would assume that people feeling a heightened sense of consciousness are better able to direct their thoughts, feelings, and behavior. They can find peace in conflict, and faith, resilience, and transcendence in struggle, because they can use their own thoughts to define the meaning of the events and experiences of their lives. They are more apt, then, to see order and meaning amid the world's chaos, giving themselves a sense of strength and optimism even in the darkest times. And the converse is true as well: when people can't control their own conscious thoughts, the tragedy of a nondirected and perhaps meaningless life ensues. People can't seem to focus their minds, emotions, and actions or consciously decide to find faith, hope, strength, or meaning in hard times.

But, of course, this only brings up more questions about how we can do all this and to what extent we can do it. It's a never-ending debate that we may never solve. The one concept about consciousness that everyone seems to agree on is that it allows us to synthesize, organize, and direct our thoughts. That's why, throughout this book, I've emphasized your power to consciously control your thoughts and attention. Whatever enables you to do that—whether it's a keen, observing mind or a little, unseen train conductor in your brain—is not that important to me. It's a field of research best left to philosophers and neuroscientists. What should excite you is simply the fact that you do have this control and that with it comes both the power and the responsibility to shape the contents of your mind and, thus, the outcomes of your life.

If all that is true, then how shall we best use our conscious ability to control our thoughts and our lives? Where shall we focus so that we can move the needle toward higher and sustained levels of happiness and engagement?

It all comes down to moving from the fascination of *how* you are conscious into a focus on *what* you should be conscious *of*. We have the ability to put whatever we desire on the conscious dashboard of our minds, so we ought to decide what we shall monitor and pay attention to. In the preceding pages, I've referred to controlling our conscious minds and thoughts in general terms. But we all are driven to transcend the obvious, and we want more from our conscious experiences. Here, then, are four specific areas to focus your consciousness on, to ensure that you're living fully aware and enlivened.

Be Conscious of Your Thoughts

Much of this book has been about consciously controlling your own thoughts, feelings, energy, experience, and meaning in life. This means being aware of such things and choosing to guide them rather than letting them unconsciously or automatically drive you. Let me give you an example of what I'm getting at, by suggesting a question you should ask yourself several times during each day: *Where shall I focus my thoughts right now?*

Note that this is *not* the same question as, *What am I currently focusing on and thinking about?* This second question is all about *being aware of* what your mind is focused on, whereas the first is about *directing* your mind.

While I'm all for being aware of what we are focusing on and thinking at any given moment, awareness is not the same as self-direction. The truth is, most of the time you are likely focusing on random things and thinking random and inconsequential thoughts. Your in-the-moment thoughts are not always necessarily that helpful in your quest to reach the next level of consciousness and control over your life. For example, in this moment, you may be randomly thinking about your first pet, and while it's helpful to be aware of this random thought, what's more likely to help you reach another level of consciousness altogether is to ask, *Where shall I focus my thoughts right now?*

I once made this question a part of one of my thirty-day personal challenges last year. I set an alarm on my phone to go off every three hours with the note, *Where shall I focus my thoughts right now?* Though I consider myself a very conscious and self-directed person, I was shocked to find out how many times during the day I was on autopilot—allowing my thinking to be controlled by impulse, habit, or external influences. As soon as I saw the reminder, I was spurred to jump back into the driver's seat of my consciousness. The result? I became much more engaged, productive, and thoughtful about deciding on the meanings of my experiences than I ever had been in my life. Don't take my word for it—give this activity a test drive yourself.

Be Conscious of Your Emotional and Physical Energies

How shall I feel right now? This is a question you should ask yourself several times a day. As with the last one, note that the question is not, *What do I feel right now?* What you are feeling at any given moment is generally a collection of millions of impulses and responses to your internal and external worlds, integrated and synthesized at the very instant you ask, *How do I feel right now?* Although how we feel at any given moment tells us a lot about our impulses and current experience, it often doesn't do much to help us heighten our own consciousness. To be more fully in control of your conscious experience, rather than let your random impulses define your feelings, you might as well define how you should be feeling.

Further, notice that the question is not, *How* should *I feel right now?* That's a question directed more by memory than by our immediate choice. In other words, the way you arrive at how you "should" feel is based on how you have felt in the past or how you think others would feel in the same situation. On the other hand, asking, *How shall I feel right now?* directs the mind to the current situation and allows you to define how you will feel in order to frame and attach meaning to any given situation.

This isn't just a question about your emotional reality, though. Our feelings are largely determined by our thoughts, of course, and also by our physical vitality. It's much easier to feel sad, frustrated, or uncertain when you're physically exhausted. Neuroscientists continue to prove that our willpower goes out the door when we feel physically drained, leading to brash or poorer-quality decisions, judgments, and actions. That's why it is so vitally important to manage your life with proper sleep, hydration, diet, and exercise.

But, alas, regardless of the upwellings of emotion we feel from our unconscious or our fatigued body, we always have a choice in determining the hues of our emotional sky. Happiness is indeed a choice. And so is feeling energized. I often prove this point at High

Performance Academy by helping people will themselves into various emotional states, sometimes without even moving a muscle. Again, the power plant doesn't *have* energy; it *generates* energy. We can choose our emotional energy in any given moment, and that is one of the greatest wonders of the human experience.

Be Conscious of Your Behavior

Our actions speak volumes about who we are, and they dictate our results in life as well as how others feel about us. When our behaviors are "off," we tend to feel terrible. If you don't take the actions that you know you should in your personal life, you feel guilty and frustrated with yourself. Take the wrong actions concerning other people, and you feel the same.

I often say that the mark of higher consciousness is always full integrity with self and deep respect for others. We can see and monitor both in how we behave consistently. Be aware of that, and bring how you are behaving and how it is affecting the world to the forefront of your mind and your conscious control.

Be Conscious of Others

Becoming a Zen master of your mental and emotional world is a bit useless in our connection-driven world if you aren't becoming more consciously attuned to others at the same time. Know thyself, yes, but know others, too. Have insight into your own life *and* seek to have insight into others' lives.

We can reach higher thought consciousness in our relationships by consistently asking ourselves, *How are others thinking and feeling in this moment, and how would I like to interact with or influence them?*

This sensing of others' perceptions and feelings, sometimes called *empathy* or *mindsight*, helps us become much more socially adept and intelligent. Now just overlay this sensing with your conscious thought about how you would like to be in this situation, and you have a recipe for more conscious and connected relationships.

Be Conscious of Your Progress

The goal of thought consciousness is to feel a greater sense of control over our internal and external worlds. But to what end? We seek higher levels of thought consciousness not just to master our world in the moment but also to move our world forward. We want to direct the outcomes of our lives and design our own legacies. If that's true, we might as well put consistent and conscious thought into how we are progressing.

Am I moving forward in life at the speed I wish to? Am I taking the necessary actions to do so? Am I managing my thoughts, feelings, behaviors, and relationships in ways that help me progress, grow, and contribute?

All this may seem like a lot to ask—to focus on so many things. I've found that it helps to think of my consciousness as the ultimate observer and driver of my life. So I like to imagine that there's a dashboard in my mind where I'm checking everything out and switching things into gear when needed. On my dashboard, I see five instrument panels, all with needles that move just like the speedometer and tachometer needles in old cars. The instrument panels I imagine are headed "Thoughts," "Feelings," "Behaviors," "Relationships," and "Speed of Progress." I keep my observant mind on these five factors in my life all the time. *Are my thoughts fueling a happy existence?* Check. *Are my feelings in tune with how I want to feel and where I want to go?* Check. *Are my behaviors making me agile, helping me move ahead, and influencing the world in a positive way?* Check. *Are my relationships reflecting who I am and what I want to be?* Check. *Am I in drive right now and speeding ahead to my full potential?* Yes? Check. Rock and roll.

Activator #2: Transcend Consciousness

Beyond mastering our own minds, most of us are driven by a sense that there is something more to figure out—something infinite, something beyond our control and imagination. At our deepest core and in our loftiest ambitions, we desire to transcend ourselves and connect with that something more. We want to experience a deeper sense of knowing about our reality and relationships with the world, the universe, and, for most of us, God or the Infinite. This sense makes us seekers of spirituality, of a connection with a higher purpose and meaning, of oneness. It's the same desire that has caused humans to create religions in hopes of touching the hem of something higher, to seek solace in nature, to reconnect, and to ask ourselves the existential questions that have driven the human search for meaning and higher purpose. This is our drive to understand and connect to a capital *C. Consciousness.*

This is something we can all do. As I've described, one of the greatest wonders of our human experience is that we can will ourselves into any emotional state we desire. You can close your eyes now and will yourself, for no particular reason, to feel a state of happiness. You can also choose to feel sad, angry, hopeful, bored, loved. This same ability allows you to will yourself into a transcendent emotional state, not just once but continually, letting yourself sense something greater than your current circumstance and connecting to a higher consciousness. Why not do just that? It's only in challenging ourselves to connect to something more than ourselves that we can feel something more than ourselves. From this connection, you will find yourself more charged and more likely to live your highest values and virtues.

Let's further explore how we can make that connection. By being present, noticing coincidence and intuition, and living in and through a state of love, we can better know that mysterious force.

230

Be Conscious of the Present Moment

As I've shared before, most people are so terribly busy and distracted that they never slow down to appreciate and take in the moment. And yet, in the present moment is where life is unfolding. And it is only here, right in the moment, that we can sense a oneness and connection with consciousness. We can't think our way into consciousness tomorrow or pull it from an experience in the past. We must experience it now, in full presence, in this very moment, the "now."

Presence means bringing your full attention and openness into now. By "full attention" we mean that you consciously seek to bring your full awareness and mental, emotional, and physical energies into the now. In the earlier drives, I described how important it is to be fully present when you're in a conversation with a person. You aren't distracted or ten steps ahead of that person, playing out the discussion as if it were some grand chess game. Instead, you're invested completely in what the other person is saying.

Yet there is a yin and yang of presence we haven't addressed yet. You are consciously engaging yourself to be fully aware and attentive to the moment, and at the same time you release yourself from any expectations—you are open to how the world is unfolding. The spiritual traditions of Buddhism and Taoism suggest that presence is a oneness with the moment, devoid of any attachments to how things should be or how things should turn out. Many even suggest that true presence is devoid of any intention at all other than to be fully open and observant in the moment.

We also haven't addressed using presence as a tool and a path to feel transcendence. I have a simple question that I ask myself dozens of times a day, usually when I begin any new experience, take any major action, or have any interaction with others. Whether walking into a new room, calling up a friend, sitting down to write, or greeting my wife when she walks in, I ask myself, *How present am I right now on a scale of one to ten?* This helps me engage and remind myself, amid our chaotic, overdesigned world, to drink in the now and seek to feel a broader connection to something larger than myself at every moment. Try it.

This is not easy work. Sometimes thoughts or attachments about the past trip me up from being present in the moment. When this happens, I ask: *What if all my negative emotions about the past are no longer relevant to this present moment and who I want to be now? What if, by viewing the past in a negative light, I'm failing to appreciate the gift of life I was given and still enjoy today? What if the past was but a moment, and now I'm in a new moment? What if this moment is only the beginning of a new and miraculous unfolding for me?*

To connect better with consciousness, you will also need to condition to withhold judgment. The judgment mechanism of our brains has become so fine-tuned by evolution that instead of experiencing the present moment, it labels our experiences as "good," "bad," "ugly," "safe," "dangerous," "happy," "sad," and so on. This serves us, of course, in almost every facet of our lives save one: it boxes in our perception of the present. We don't fully experience the now, because we're so busy labeling it. This is akin to all those vacationers you see in front of landmarks or scenic vistas who never even look at them, because they're so busy getting out their cameras. They take the snapshot, but they never experience the view. We have to learn to stop labeling and categorizing and fixing our will on every second of the day and, instead, *be at peace with and fully present with what is.*

This might sound contradictory given that most of this book has been about shaping our lives. But being self-directed and being at peace with the past and the moment are not mutually exclusive. I can be ready and willing to improve my life and yet at total peace with what my life is now. It's not necessary, as some argue, for me to generate tremendous feelings of pain and frustration over my current life experiences in order to propel me to change. In fact, I think that's horrible advice—certainly not spiritual advice. Few positive things ever resulted over the long term when driven by anger, frustration, or hurt. I say, instead, to accept what is in this moment, to fully acknowledge and appreciate that it all has unfolded in this way for a reason and that an even greater door is opening for you, at this very second, to something more magical and exciting than you could ever fathom.

Be Conscious of Coincidence and Intuition

If you're in the now and you're seeking to connect with consciousness, you tend to notice that things and people appear in your life just in time or for a reason that seems to make sense (whether in the moment or over time). You've been trying to think of an idea for your next product, and while you're strolling along outside, fully in the now, the idea just pops into your mind. Or you're at a networking event and sense a very strong feeling to go meet someone across the room whom you've never met—you just feel a strong impulse to speak with the person. These are moments of what some have called a "consciousness coincidence."

Coincidence is defined as something happening simultaneously with something else. *The World English Dictionary* defines it as "a chance occurrence of events remarkable either for being simultaneous or for apparently being connected."

Of course, the word "chance" is open to debate by those who feel that consciousness is introducing something into our lives for a specific reason. Perhaps it's not just chance that you bumped into your long-lost love at the coffee shop—maybe it's fate. Regardless of whether we believe in chance, fate, or some combination of both, we all can benefit from being more attuned to how and why things are being introduced to us in the now.

For me, the greatest practice of presence involves noticing coincidences of "chance encounters" with other people. If, at the airport,

I run into someone I haven't seen in years, I bring my full presence into that moment and seek to connect with the energy of the experience. I also try to "follow" the moment closely, listening to my intuition in the moment. *This person has been reintroduced into my life at this precise moment. I wonder why. I'm going to pay attention and give this conversation my full presence and see where it leads us.*

Not everyone believes in coincidence, of course, seeing instead a universe that is unfolding at random. Regardless, to feel a heightened connection with consciousness, whether we believe it to be something omnipotent or not, we have to pay attention to what the moment is serving up in our lives. Being on the lookout for coincidences helps us do that.

Directly related to coincidence is the concept of intuition. Intuition is always a coincidence in that it's a "gut feeling" that coincides with something else. You think about your mom and have an intuitive sense that you should call her. (Do it, by the way.) Or you have a strong feeling to get off the Jetway just as you are about to board a plane. (Ditto.)

In surveying my audiences from around the globe, I've found that most people feel they are losing touch with their intuition. That's easy to understand, because many people are so focused on tomorrow that they can't feel anything in the moment. The only fix for this is to become more present, stay in the now and release your planning mind and all its expectations, and just sense your surroundings.

Be Conscious of Love

All the world's religions have love as their central—and, most often, highest—virtue and value. Most faiths suggest that we were born of love, that our purpose is to love, and that we will return to love. This, then, is something we ought to be paying close attention to.

You already know the value of love. You've been seeking it all your life. But the real question is how much you've allowed yourself to *sense* it and *live* it. That's a pretty big distinction. Seekers of love tend to be needy, searching for ways to fill up their cup and feel connected and cared for. These are human drives, of course, and we all pursue such things. But there is a way to feel more in contact with consciousness. And that's by being present to the love that is already all around us and within us, and becoming one with that love by living it.

Being conscious of the love around us sounds like a fairly bizarre concept, since most of us think that for us to experience love, someone must "give" it to us. Sadly, most people's experience of love comes only when they feel loved by another. But what if love is a bigger concept? What if love itself is the unifying force holding the universe together and uniting all of us? As grand and high-flying as that may sound, it seems that's what most spiritual teachings have suggested for thousands of years.

Sensing the love around us is powerful, but becoming one with it and living through it is a whole other level of consciousness. If we all aim to get love in our lives, why not give it? Living from this place changes our entire focus from "Ask and you shall receive" to "Give and you shall receive." But we can go further yet. Love is all around us, and it has been given freely, so perhaps we should give love without expecting anything in return.

If all this resonates with you, try, today and for the rest of your life, to be more loving. Notice the love that exists all around you. Exude love to others. Think from the place of love before making decisions. Talk about love openly. If you can do that, your life will come *alive*. As Pierre Teilhard de Chardin said, "Someday, after mastering winds, waves, tides and gravity, we shall harness the energy of love; and for the second time in the history of the world, man will have discovered fire."

Being more conscious of our presence, coincidence, our intuition, and love are ways that we can better know and explore the consciousness all around us.

Activator #3: Live in Wonder

When I stood atop a crumpled car hood on a Caribbean island, staring toward the heavens in thanks for my second chance in life, I felt a profound sense of awe and wonder about the world. I sensed there was something magical about that night and about life in general. That feeling has never left me. And it's one reason I always maintain my charge.

When you are in awe and appreciation of the magic of the universe, then it's easy to feel connected to it. Just as you feel closer to your spouse when you are astonished by her or his generosity or when you appreciate who he or she is and how much your spouse loves you, so, too, can you feel closer to consciousness.

These days, it's easy to get detached from all the marvels around us. We get antsy when our cell phones drop a call and forget the magical fact that the signal going from the little square box in our hand must travel to some distant cell tower or satellite in *space*, then through the air at tremendous speeds, then somehow, out of *seven billion* people, find the *right* person's little square box on the other end. When it comes to our own technological advancement, we are perhaps the most oblivious and unappreciative generation in history. And if we cannot marvel at our own advancement, it's likely that we will have difficulty marveling at that of an unspecified entity or force that we've never seen.

To sense consciousness, we must slow down and notice the marvels unfolding all around us. We must allow ourselves to be amazed and astonished by the flow of the river, the blueness of the sky, the smile of the child, the stillness of a peaceful morning. Yet we must not simply wait for something to generate a sense of awe in us. We can rise above being stimulus-response animals and cultivate our own emotions, steering our free will into creating a sense of awe within our being. In this moment, I can simply decide to feel awe at the wonders of this universe, and in doing so, I feel closer to consciousness.

It *is* amazing that we all are alive in such an ever-expanding universe. Here we sit, on a tiny blue sphere that spins about one thousand miles per hour and is moving around the sun at 65,000 miles per hour. But our tiny blue ball of life is but a speck in a cosmos stretching many billions of light-years. We have no clue where the universe even ends, and if we did, we would never be sure of it. As Archytas, a fourth-century BCE philosopher, once asked, "Supposing that I came to the outer limits of the universe. If I now thrust out a stick, what would I find?"

The sheer expansiveness of the universe, and our improbable ability to thrive within it, should astound us all. But a greater unknown also moves through us, giving us life and spirit, taking it away. What is it that gives us our life energy? God? The universe? Random luck? These questions should intrigue us, and we ought to meet them with our full wonder and reverence in living a Charged Life.

Tonight, when I wrote these words, I had a sense that my father was near. I meet that feeling with a sense of true wonder and appreciation. He is gone and I miss him deeply, yet I feel his energy very close to me from time to time. Perhaps the universe is such a wondrous place that our charge carries on forever.

A Final Thought

The Charged Life urges us to transcend our normal ways of thinking and shift to a higher gear by better controlling the dashboard of our own consciousness. It also challenges us to find a higher purpose and meaning in our own human experience and to rise above our own circumstance and connect with something greater than ourselves, to stretch beyond the mundane to the magical.

It's a different kind of life, to be sure—a much more consciously designed existence. But what else is there? Shall we let our impulses alone control us, or shall we direct our attention and activities to a higher state of motivation, meaning, and morality? Shall we let the world go spinning past us, or shall we use our presence to slow it down, take it in, appreciate the *magic* of it all? And through each day and up to the very end, when we sense those last moments of life, shall we simply and casually wonder about the force of something beyond us, or shall we slip the bonds of our limited senses and choose to connect with and live through divine love? The choice, as it has always been, is yours.

CHARGE POINTS

1. If I were more aware and directive of my consciousness in life, my life would change in these ways . . .

2. To connect with a higher consciousness on a more regular basis, I could . . .

3. The things that inspire my wonder about the world and my place in it include . . .

Conclusion

There are just 10 human drives, and yet neither you nor I will ever completely master them. We will come to better understand them, we will struggle and improve in activating them, yet we will never know complete victory over all of them at once, or even just one. Concluding a book by saying we cannot win may seem odd, but it rings true to the theme of this work—the real gift is the journey you take as you strive to get better and deeper into your life. Living a fully Charged Life demands constant choice, presence, focus, stretching, growth, and mastery. Enjoying the blessings of being energized, engaged, and enthusiastic requires hard work, struggle, and a commitment most will never have.

And yet I believe you do. We've traveled far together, rounding the bases of our drives to have more control, competence, congruence, caring, and connection; we've swung for the fences in advancing our lives through our drives for change, challenge, creative expression, contribution, and consciousness. Simply knowing the playing field of our own human condition sets us up to better succeed in the grandest game we will ever know—life.

The game will be harder than you imagined, as will activating these 10 human drives consciously and consistently. That is why I say you will not know complete victory. But this is not a bad thing. As a society, we must stop looking at those things that are labeled as "hard" as also being "bad." If anything, in these pages, we've learned that "easy" and "comfortable" are often detractors from a fully Charged Life. It is only in challenging ourselves that we feel alive once more, energized and engaged in pushing ourselves toward a brighter future, one which lights our hearts and souls with a brilliant enthusiasm unknown to the masses of the caged or comfortable. It is in this relentless challenging of ourselves to be bolder, better, stronger, happier, and more fulfilled that we recognize our own limitations and break through into a life beyond our own imaginations. The struggle is worth it.

I won't rehash old ground here, recapping all the drives and activators; I want you to read this book multiple times, spilling ink on journals and wearing keys down on your computer as you take notes, dream, plan. You can find all the resources I've created for you on your journey at www.TheChargeBook.com/resources. From there, your work now will be in giving yourself permission to live fully expressed and in pushing yourself every single day to have more *life* in your life. As you do, remember to take that work beyond yourself and engage others with an intent to charge their lives as well. The work will be worth it. In the days ahead, regardless of what you've learned, you will rise some days and feel in control of your life so completely that you wonder how you were ever weak or unsure; and there will be days in which control is stripped away. That is life. And it is worth it.

So what does the path ahead hold for you? Surely, you will find more energy and enthusiasm by focusing on your internal charge in life. But there is more. You will also discover a greater clarity about life, a deeper sense of meaning, a more profound appreciation and respect for others and the gifts you've been given. Feeling charged leads one to feeling grateful. What could feel better than to feel more thankful for our own lives?

As we finish here, nothing in the outer world may have changed. The same issues and problems and opportunities and people will likely still surround you when you close these covers. My hope is that something within you changed, that there is a new and lasting commitment for a better life, that if anything, you've found a spark here strong enough to someday light a wild fire within you so hot and so untamable that no trouble can extinguish it nor can any man or woman on earth douse it with disbelief.

If I am to leave you with anything, it is in revealing one more drive. The eleventh human drive. Unlike the previous 10, this drive has not likely directed your entire life so palpably. Unlike the others, it is not the subject of academic tomes, centuries of philosophic debate, or neuroscientists' prying machines. Yet it is a distinctly human desire that makes all our efforts and struggles and hard-fought gains in activating the other drives so worthwhile. It's a drive that unites us when we see an athlete exert his or her best, when our teams at work meet the impossible deadline, when we witness a hero emerge from the inferno, when our children demonstrate character and aid others, and when we, ourselves, having slogged through our own insecurities, doubts, and dilemmas, suddenly emerge ahead and clean and pure, astounding those around us and even ourselves. That drive, activated only in witness of our best efforts and character, and activated only when we've committed to and achieved something worthwhile, something meaningful, something in service to something larger than we, is *Celebration*.

Living a Charged Life requires much of you. You must be more conscious about designing your days and activating your drives. You must boldly adventure out into the world again, stretching yourself in pursuit of greater joys and enthusiasms. You must soar above your own shortcomings. You must express your highest self. And it is only in doing this, out there, in a world rich with choice and challenge and fear and freedom, that your greatest gifts will be expressed and where your life will become one of constant celebration.

The world will indeed celebrate your efforts. Listen. It is out there that destiny calls. Be bold and ready yourself. It is time to charge once again.

Acknowledgments

To my amazement, this is my fourth book. People always ask, "What's the hardest part of writing a book?" My answer and my reality remain the same: the acknowledgments section. It's impossible to thank all those who have led and supported me in arriving to this moment. One of my greatest joys in writing this section, though, is in seeing that everyone I've thanked in my previous books is still in my life. Growth friends until the end.

I begin once more by continuing to feel deeply grateful for life's golden ticket—the second chance I was given by God. I live each day to earn that blessing, and in my efforts to live fully, love openly, and make a difference, I am most thankful for His love and guidance.

This book is also once again dedicated in part to my father, Mel Burchard. We lost you too soon, Dad, but we were lucky to have you as long as we did, and we will carry your charge forever.

To Mom, David, Bryan, and Helen—I love you all. You've always believed in me and let me live my own life, and you've inspired me by living your own as well. I am charged because of your love and support. Mom, you will always be taken care of.

To my eternal sunshine, Denise. I remain in awe of the love we share, and it is that love that lights my life brighter and brighter every day. Eight years, Sunshine, and not one day has gone by that I haven't felt a giddy and grateful charge in my heart to be with you.

To the guys and "all my friends!" I don't know how many times our crazy adventures have almost killed one of us, but damn, it's been fun. I hope that, despite my busyness and track record of missed calls, you never bucket me in the maintenance-friend category. For your lifelong friendship, I love you: Jason Sorenson, Gwenda Houston, Dave Ries, Adam Standiford, Ryan Grepper, Steve Roberts, Jesse Brunner, Matt and Mark Hiesterman, Jeff Buszmann, Jessy Villano Falk, Brian Simonson, Dave Smith, Nick Dedominic, Jenny Owens, Dana Fetrow, Phil Bernard, and Stephan and Mira Blendstrup.

The reason you are reading this book is because my high school journalism teacher, Linda Ballew, inspired within me a love of writing and a drive to share intelligent conversation with the world. Ballewby, I hope in your eyes I've done okay on the latter.

Once again thanks to my friends and former coworkers at Accenture who taught me about business, excellence, and professionalism, especially Jenny Chan, Mary Bartlett, Teri Babcock, and Janet Hoffman.

I have no idea how to thank Scott Hoffman, my agent and the best in the publishing business. My friend, look at what we've done together. I'm honored to do it all with your guidance and friendship. Scott is the reason my books are around the world.

To Roger Freet and the whole team at HarperOne who believed in me and published *Life's Golden Ticket*. That book is still my baby. Thanks for believing in me when I myself was just a baby in the industry. Thank you to Michael Carr, who has helped copyedit the first draft of all of my books and always helps me find the proper words and places for my commas, like the one you just saw.

My story of becoming an expert in the motivation and human-performance space began by being a student and seeker. Thanks to these incredible teachers, who in the months and years following my car accident at the age of nineteen changed my life: Tony Robbins, Paulo Coehlo, James Redfield, Brian Tracy, Stephen Covey, Mark Victor Hansen, Jack Canfield, John Gray, Wayne Dyer, Debbie

Ford, Benjamin Hoff, Og Mandino, Marianne Williamson, John Gottman, Nathaniel Branden, Phillip McGraw, Mitch Albom, Les Brown, Deepak Chopra, David Bach, and other legends both living and past. I'm honored to now count many of you as friends and peers.

Tony Robbins deserves significant credit here for inspiring me to dramatically change the quality of my life following my accident. I still remember hearing your voice in my car and one day thinking, *Maybe someday I'll get to be that voice for others, and maybe someday I'll get to thank this guy.* Thanks, Tony, for everything.

In recent years, many of these experts shared invaluable life lessons and marketing ideas, support, or training that helped me spread my message far and wide: Rick Frishman, Steve and Bill Harrison, Jeff Walker, Jim Kwik, Frank Kern, Bill Harris, Srikumar Rao, Eben Pagan, Jay Abraham, Jeff Johnson, Mike Koenigs, Seth Godin, Andy Jenkins, Joe Polish, Ryan Deiss, Tim Ferriss, Yanik Silver, Roger Love, Mike Filsaime, Paul Colligan, Brad Fallon, Garrett Gunderson, Richard Rossi, Trey Smith, Dean Graziosi, Jay Conrad Levinson, David Hancock, Darren Hardy, Daniel Amen, Ken Kleinberg, Bo Eason, Chris Atwood, Tellman Knudson, Randy Garn, Tony Hsieh, T. Harv Eker, Dean Jackson, Brian Kurtz, Rich Schefren, Brian Johnson, Armand Morin, John Carlton, Vishen Lakhiani, Don Crowther, Jason Van Orden, Jason Deitch, Dan Sullivan, John Assaraf, Paula Abdul. Thanks to you all.

It's impossible to thank everyone who has helped me share my message, so I apologize to all my supporters, affiliates, fans, clients, and friends not listed here. I appreciate you. To my private clients— you know who you are and you know you are loved. Serving you charges me every day.

My team makes all this possible. Jenni Robbins, you are still the most talented, detailed, efficient, collaborative, and remarkable professional and friend I've ever known. I'm glad we get to charge the world together. To the rest of the crew, thanks will never be enough: Denise McIntyre, Travis Shields, Karen Lo, Heather Moffett, Lauren Davis, Audrey Hagen, Shawn Royster, John Josepho, Mel Abraham, Roberto Secades. Thanks, too, to our past teammates and countless and incredibly dedicated volunteers who enliven our events and inspire our customers.

To my new team and friends at Free Press—wow, wow, wow. Thank you for bringing this work into the world and being such an incredibly supportive, savvy, and personable publisher. I have deep respect for you all. Dominick Anfuso got behind this book, and that's why you're reading it—he and Martha Levin are the top reasons I joined the Free Press family. Dominick, in all you went through while we were working on this project, you remained steady, present, helpful, attentive, ever the leader and good man. I'm amazed at what you and Leah Miller did in editing this book and helping me find its essence. To the rest of the team, I owe you so much and am loving this journey with you: Martha Levin (thank you for believing in me!), Suzanne Donahue, Carisa Hays, Larry Hughes, Sydney Tanigawa, Emily Jarrett, Tom Spain.

Finally, to you, the reader: I'm charged daily thinking that I've gotten to share my voice with you. I hope to hear your voice one day. Please keep up with me on Facebook and let me know how you're doing. Now . . . *Charge!*

Index

About the Author

Brendon Burchard is the founder of High Performance Academy and the bestselling author of *Life's Golden Ticket*. He is also author of #1 *New York Times* and #1 *USA Today* bestselling book *The Millionaire Messenger*. For these works, Brendon has become one of the top motivation and marketing trainers in the world, and his books, videos, newsletters, products, and appearances now inspire nearly two million people a month worldwide.

Brendon was blessed to receive life's golden ticket—a second chance—after surviving a car accident in a developing country. Since then, he has dedicated his life to helping individuals, teams, and organizations find their charge, share their voices, and make a greater difference in the world.

Brendon is regularly seen on public television, and he has been in media appearances on *Anderson Cooper, ABC World News*, NPR stations, *Oprah and Friends*, and other popular programs and outlets like *SUCCESS* magazine, Forbes.com, and the *Huffington Post*. As one of the most in-demand trainers of our time, he has shared the stage with the Dalai Lama, Sir Richard Branson, Tony Hsieh, Tony Robbins, Wayne Dyer, Stephen Covey, Deepak Chopra, Marianne Williamson, David Bach, John Gray, Brian Tracy, Keith Ferrazzi, Harv Eker, Les Brown, Debbie Ford, Jack Canfield, and more. Brendon's client list reads like a Who's Who roster in the corporate and celebrity worlds, and his seminars have been attended by executives and entrepreneurs from more than fifty countries. Brendon's hallmark live events include High Performance Academy, Experts Academy, World's Greatest Speaker Training, and 10X Wealth & Business.

Meet Brendon and receive free training and resources, at BrendonBurchard.com.